Our Call to Extraordinary Ministry in Extraordinary Times

Our Call to Extraordinary Ministry in Extraordinary Times

A Coming Reformation...

Randy Fisk

*Our Call to Extraordinary Ministry in Extraordinary Times –
A Coming Reformation...*

Copyright © 2015 by Randy Fisk

Published by Second Ref Press, North Aurora, Illinois 60542
www.secondrefpress.com

ISBN: 978-0-692-46439-7

All Scripture quotations, unless otherwise indicated, are taken from the HOLY BIBLE, NEW INTERNATIONAL VERSION®. NIV®. Copyright © 1973, 1978, 1984 by International Bible Society. Used by permission of Zondervan. All rights reserved.

Scripture references marked KJV are from the King James Version of the Bible. Those marked NKJV are from the New King James Version®. Copyright © 1982 by Thomas Nelson, Inc. Used by permission. All rights reserved.

All rights reserved. This book may not be reproduced in any form for commercial gain or profit. Copying short quotations or occasional pages is permitted and encouraged. Otherwise seek the permission of the author.

For inquiries about the book or availability to teach, the author may be contacted at RandyFisk333@gmail.com.

Cover design by Holly Fisk and Keith Lang.

Edited by Mandy Fisk.

Printed in the United States of America

Dedicated to:

***Judah**—*
Future Lion of Worship

***Rayah**—*
Who will Sing, be Strong, and do Exploits

*and **Faith**—*
Whose Soft Words will Move Mountains

Acknowledgements

I would like to thank my wonderful wife Mary for her encouragement, perceptiveness, and the journey we walk together which helped me write this book. I would also like to thank my children, Holly, Becky, and Mandy, and son-in-law, Keith, for their insights and for being the amazing people they are. Becky, the songs you and Keith record are such an inspiration to me—the Holy Spirit hovers over them. I also appreciate my many friends, colleagues, and pastors (notably Mike Smith) who pushed me forward to know more and more of God. Many thanks, too, to Mandy Fisk for the thoughtful and perceptive way she edited this book. Also, special thanks to Holly Fisk for her awesome cover painting and to Keith Lang in the way he used it to create the cover of this book. I also want to express my gratitude to my friend Robby Dawkins—a true Braveheart and inspirer of many to go forward in the face of battle. Finally, I would like to thank my Lord and God, who always gives me more than I ask. God, You are truly amazing.

Contents

Introduction 11

1	Characteristics of the Coming Revival	15
2	Walking in the Now and Not Yet	19
3	Who Are You?	31
4	Authority	37
5	Identity	45
6	Jesus' Identity and Ours	53
7	The First and Second Reformations	61
8	Tenacity	67
9	Fellowship with the Trinity	75
10	Three Elements of Ministry	81
11	Ministry in the Last Days	93

Appendix: A Tale of Two Sisters 107

Bibliography 113

About the Author 115

Introduction

For some reason, the notion of reformation has always intrigued me. Thirty-four years ago, while attending seminary in St. Louis, I remember standing in front of a statue of Martin Luther, trying to get inside the head of this remarkable man who led the church into a renewed grasp of certain truths, heading the church into a brave new direction. The trouble with trying to get inside someone's head, however, is that their ideas get inside yours. During that same period of time, I read about what some have called the *Second Reformation*. This is a reformation, yet to come, where *ministry* will come into the hands of the people. John Stott touched upon this in his book, *The Message of Ephesians*. He said, "If the sixteenth century recovered the 'priesthood of all believers' (every Christian enjoying through Christ a direct access to God), perhaps the twentieth century will recover the 'ministry of all believers' (every Christian receiving from Christ a privileged ministry to men)." (p.168).

The thought of such a reformation has been with me ever since. In my first book, *The Presence, Power and Heart of God—Partnering in His Ministry*, I wrote how that reformation snuck up on me when I witnessed the Holy Spirit moving and authoring His ministry in many of my friends. I wrote that book to help us follow the Holy Spirit's lead in whatever He might have us do, whether it is ministering healing, speaking His words, or showing someone the way to a life-giving relationship with God. I have seen many people step into this, which I continue to find awe-inspiring. Yet I still long to see this reformation sweep over the church with the magnitude I know it can.

I can feel a move of the Spirit at our doorstop, however, and a reformation like I am describing is part of it. I believe the ministry involved will be extraordinary, both in the number of people doing it as well as the remarkable things that will happen. But I also believe the season in which this happens will be extraordinary in many different ways—not always comfortable, but extraordinary. (Please note that I am not saying that the "ordinary" things we do for the Lord do not count. They most certainly do. However, even these things are extraordinary in God's eyes and may have extraordinary results when we do them. The part we play is often profoundly simple: a word of the Lord, an extension of our hand, or a deed of kindness, but it can precipitate an awesome work of the Lord. Even small things, done with great love, can change the world.)

A few years ago, God began speaking some truths to me that at first seemed disconnected. Then, however, they began forming into a pattern that started shaking my world. I soon came to realize that this was the key to seeing the Second Reformation come in a major way. At the same time, I came to see a people who were already in motion with much of what the Lord was showing me. Furthermore, I began to see that underlying this was actually the same revelation that Martin Luther first came to realize in the beginning of his reformation, almost exactly 500 years ago. I will speak more about that later.

As if this were not enough, this came on the heels of a conversation with my mother some months earlier, who told me she had discovered that some of my direct ancestors had been reformers. She even found that, in early America, a cousin of one of my ancestors had been imprisoned for trying to start a prayer meeting outside the four walls of the church. (The church was often very protective of its turf back then.) A passion to get ministry outside of the four walls of the church has long been something that burns in me as well.

You might think that I felt some sort of twinge about this in my childhood. Not so. When I was young, going to Sunday school and church seemed like a chore. But even then, I had a hunger and an inner drive pushing me to something more than I knew. It wasn't until my mid-twenties, when I met my wife Mary, that I started finding that something more.

At that time I began to read the Bible with new eyes, seeing even familiar stories in a new, fascinating light. For example, you can hear a story like Daniel in the lions' den as a youngster and, as you get a little older, start dismissing it because you never really heard the entire story. Maybe, you think, Daniel survived because the lions were not that hungry, or were weak, or had a friendly streak. It wasn't until I read it later that I saw that, after Daniel survived, his enemies were thrown into the den and the lions tore them bone from bone, eating them before their bodies had a chance to reach the bottom of the den. Granted, that would be too scary to teach a five-year old, but I couldn't help but wonder if someone had been leaving out essential parts. Even more essential than the gory details, however, is whether we are leaving out the lesson that *we* can be a Daniel. Or that God can supernaturally move in response to *us*. Or that, like Daniel, we can demonstrate that God is like no other, as we partner with Him to show His power and presence to a world that has dismissed Him as missing, weak, or aloof.

James tells us that "Elijah was a man just like us. He prayed earnestly that it would not rain, and it did not rain on the land for three and a half years. Again he prayed, and the heavens gave rain, and the earth produced its crops." (James 5:17-18). Why did James say this if not to encourage *us* that we can have an identity, authority, and ministry like Elijah, if we would but reach for it? Yet how many would dare even try this, let alone teach it? However, we would dare do it if we knew who we are in the Lord.

Knowing who we are in God is one of the truths that has been turning my life upside down lately. I have come to realize this is not a side issue—it is one of the central truths of the Christian faith. It is the key for the extraordinary ministry I will be describing. It is worthy of a reformation. It was, in fact, the spark and part and parcel of the first reformation, once you look for it there. Once again, it is sparking another reformation. When it is uncovered, it has the potential to set our lives and the life of the church ablaze. Lord, let this fire fall!

1
Characteristics of the Coming Revival

There is a phenomenal move of God starting to dawn. Time will tell if I am right, but I feel history is in the making. If you have not yet seen what I am about to describe, you will. It will come with the power of a tsunami, simultaneous with a shaking of the world, changing everything. It is available to all who would latch onto the Spirit. It is beginning with waves that we can now see, but the secret is that we must learn to ride these current waves, for only then can we be on top of the huge ones when they come crashing in.

From what I see, there are three major characteristics of the coming revival. I will summarize them here, and then expand upon each in subsequent chapters.

Ministering Like Jesus

Even now there is a renewed interest in healing, prophetic ministry, God's presence, and inviting people to come into His Kingdom—doing all that Jesus did, and doing it with His heart of love. However, just hearing about these things or experiencing them solely within the four walls of the church is no longer enough. There is a hunger to see this affect the outside world. Those who are being raised up are not satisfied with simply hearing about it—they have to do it!

Authority and Identity

God is renewing an emphasis on authority, particularly as it relates to the realms of healing and intercession. Closely connected with that, and underpinning everything else about the move of God which is underway, is coming to know who we are. In other words, God is establishing our identity. This changes everything about the way we think, walk, and do what Jesus did.

Tenacity

Many young people (or young at heart) are catching this vision. And they are contending for it. They are tenacious in the pursuit of God and this vision. They are very honoring toward all the church, but they know it is important to be in fellowship with others who are contending for this vision too. Therefore, as we become holders of the vision, we will soon be joined by a band of others whose hearts are to push forward the frontiers of the Kingdom.

Such a heart is evidenced in Matthew 11:12 "… the violent take [the Kingdom] by force" (KJV). Or, as it is expressed in the Amplified Bible: "… a share in the heavenly kingdom is sought with most ardent zeal and intense exertion." It takes a forceful grasp to lay hold of the forceful advancing of the Kingdom, and it takes tenacity to keep pushing ahead. This wave of God is raising up an army of warriors, like David's mighty men, who display valiant perseverance in promoting the cause of their King.

The Scope of this Move of God

What I have been feeling for some time is that this will touch virtually every denomination. Looking at the Body of Christ as a tree, you can place the denominations on it in the order that they were birthed, with the Jewish people near the roots, the Roman Catholics and Orthodox near the trunk, the Lutherans, Anglicans, etc. somewhere above that, other major denominations above them, and the more recent movements toward the outside. It seems that the revivals and movements of the past have formed new parts of the outside of the tree. What is coming, I feel, is going to be different. The streams of revival will come into the entire tree, even culminating in the Jewish roots. As this happens, the entire tree will be enriched. Some have been strategically placed, having connections to parts of the tree above and below them. These God will use for the streams to flow. We will all come to appreciate how this outpouring is way bigger than something affecting just a part of the tree.

> **God is shaking not only the denominations, but world religions.**

God is shaking not only the denominations, but world religions. There is a remarkable occurrence that has been happening for a while now, where members of different world religions, such as Muslims, are having dreams of Jesus and are coming to Him by supernatural means. There have been stories of Christians whom God has sent to give prophetic words to Imams and other religious leaders, only to have found that God had already spoken to them, those words confirming to these people what they had already experienced. Darren Wilson's movie *Father of Lights* captures this in its stunning reality, as the camera follows individuals led by God to leaders of other faiths whom God had already prepared for His encounters.

As amazing as *Father of Lights* is, however, what you don't see is even more amazing—the astounding words and works of the Christians it highlights are actually multiplied thousands of times over by a myriad of others who are doing the very same things. This raising up of an army of God is what I call the *Second Reformation*: ministry coming into the people's hands. It is happening now. Although not everyone in this army has the exact same gift sets and is used the same way, virtually everything Jesus did is being done. They are demonstrating His reality, power, and heart. And they are demonstrating how every Christian can be involved in the remarkable things that Jesus does.

2
Walking in the Now and Not Yet

There is no perfect way to organize all that is in this book, so I will present it as it happened to me. This chapter is how it began—the first piece in the puzzle.

After finishing my second book, *The Amazing Word of God*, one of the paragraphs I had written kept milling in my mind. I knew it was true, but never thought much about it before writing it. It is this: "We live in a temporal world, whereas the things of God are eternal—when God speaks, His words do not fade away but remain forever. So His promises are as powerful today as when He first spoke them." (p. 86). In other words, the fact that God is timeless casts a different light on His words—they exist eternally.

Having a background in physics, I have always been intrigued by the subject of time. It can be thought of as a fourth dimension, but one in which we are all moving together. In one sense it is like a book. A book is simply a collection of words, but when we read it, our mind superimposes a past (where we have read), a present (where we are currently reading), and a future (what we have yet to read). Yet we can stand back and see that it is just a string of words. When it comes to reality, of course, we have no choice but to flow in time like everyone else. God, however, can stand back from it and see the beginning just as clearly as the end. He is outside of time. (One might ask whether God is writing it as we are reading it, which I think is partially true, but that is beyond my comprehension!)

What is certain, however, is that God's perspective of the world is very different from our own. This perspective affects everything about Him, and it is fascinating to see that the Bible actually has this timeless perspective captured in its pages. When Jesus was called the Alpha and the Omega, He was not just at one time the Alpha (the beginning) and at another time will be the Omega (the end), but simultaneously is the Alpha and the Omega. This fact stands outside of time.

In subsequent chapters I want to talk about our identity and ministry. It is not surprising that knowing who we are begins with knowing who God is. However, could it really be that something as unfathomable as the timelessness of God (or, for that matter, *any* of His characteristics) have any connection with who we, as mere finite beings, are? Does it have a connection with our ministry? Amazingly it does.

The Timeless Perspective of God

In the prophetic books of the Old Testament, when God gave promises of what was to come, He often spoke from His perspective of timelessness, seeing the far future as clearly as the near. When He spoke, the near and distant future were often intertwined—some verses pertaining to the near future, the next verses to the far future, then back again (such as in Isaiah 7-9). For example, sometimes He would speak of the coming release of Israel's captivity interspersed with a picture of the freedom His Son would bring hundreds of years later. And threaded within these might be the final victory realized at the second coming of Jesus. This intertwining of time frames often led to a lack of understanding of just what a prophetic word was about. Sometimes a prophetic word had multiple applications. For example, Isaiah 51 says this:

> Therefore the redeemed of the LORD shall return, and come with singing unto Zion; and everlasting joy shall be upon their head. (Isaiah 51:11, KJV)

The immediate fulfillment is the return of Israel from its captivity in Babylon. Yet it also is a foreshadowing of the redemption won for us in Jesus' first coming. And, at the same time, it is a picture of the joy that the redeemed will experience in His second coming. (Note: I am sticking with obvious applications, a good approach to interpret Scripture.)

> **When He spoke, the near and distant future were often intertwined.**

Some have likened this to looking at mountain peaks. From a distance, two mountain peaks can look like one, but it is not until you drive past one of them that you can see that the other peak is much farther away than the first. The Old Testament prophets often bounced from one mountain to the other and back again, describing what they were seeing without distinguishing the actual sequence of events. We are now at a time when we can tell one mountain from the other because one is behind us and the other is ahead. The prophecies were written this way because the prophets gazed upon the revelation of a timeless God.

Foreshocks

Another aspect of God's timelessness is that, not only in His writings, but in life, there are often foretastes of momentous events He is about to do. Just as earthquakes have aftershocks, with God there are often foreshocks to things that lie ahead.

The death and resurrection of Jesus were the most momentous events in human history, and each had their foretastes in times preceding them. Many Old Testament prophecies gave future pictures of Jesus' death, sometimes involving the smallest of details. Isaiah 53 is perhaps the most notable example of this. The story of Abraham who was called to sacrifice his son Isaac (Genesis 22) is another remarkable fore-type of the death of God's Son, which we can see from a father's perspective.

> **Just as earthquakes have aftershocks, with God, there are often foreshocks to things that lie ahead.**

The resurrection of Jesus (and, one day, of us all) had many foretastes. The dry bones prophecy of Ezekiel 37 is an example. It ends as follows:

> Therefore prophesy and say to them: "This is what the Sovereign LORD says: O my people, I am going to open your graves and bring you up from them; I will bring you back to the land of Israel. Then you, my people, will know that I am the LORD, when I open your graves and bring you up from them." (Ezekiel 37:12-13)

This is another example of a prophecy which spoke of a fulfillment in the hearers' day, a foretaste of the resurrection of Jesus, and an ultimate fulfillment in our resurrection, when Jesus will come again.

As Jesus' death and resurrection grew closer, we see a foretaste of His resurrection in the resurrection of Lazarus when Jesus said, "I am the resurrection and the life." (John 11:25). However, at Jesus' death, where the price for our lives was paid, the resurrection foretastes built into a crescendo, including this, which was a literal foreshock of the resurrection power to come:

> And when Jesus had cried out again in a loud voice, he gave up his spirit. At that moment the curtain of

> the temple was torn in two from top to bottom. The earth shook and the rocks split. The tombs broke open and the bodies of many holy people who had died were raised to life. They came out of the tombs, and after Jesus' resurrection they went into the holy city and appeared to many people. (Matthew 27:50-53)

It was as if, when Jesus died and His blood dropped upon the ground, a wave of life—of resurrection power—was released. Even as a foreshock it shook the earth and raised people from the dead. That "wave" (which, of course, was the presence of God) raised Jesus to life and continued to spread. It transformed lives wherever it went and continues to this day. I bear witness—it gave me life—it transformed every area of my being which I did not know was dead until I compared it with the life which now swept over me.

This wave will continue until one amazing day when our mortal bodies, living or dead, will experience its power to transform them from one type to quite another. It is interesting that Scripture speaks of Jesus' resurrection as a foretaste of our own resurrection, fulfilled when He comes again:

> But Christ has indeed been raised from the dead, the firstfruits of those who have fallen asleep. (1 Corinthians 15:20)

Bookends

Sometimes God orders human history as if He is writing the beginning of a chapter with the end in mind. Thus the beginning and end of an occurrence become bookends to what lies in the middle, the beginning containing foretastes of what is in the end. Such is the mark of God's authorship on the order of things.

For example, consider the life of God's Son. When Jesus was born, He was wrapped in swaddling clothes (Luke 2:7, 12). Swaddling clothes were long strips of linen wrapped tightly over the baby to make the baby feel secure. But why was attention given to this detail? At the end of Jesus life it says this: "Peter, however, got up and ran to the tomb. Bending over, he saw the strips of linen lying by themselves" (Luke 24:12a). Again, long strips of linen. Such detail, authored by God, serve as bookends to what He wants us to see. The timeless God, who at the beginning also sees the end, does things this way.

> **It is not surprising that the Bible - human history itself - would have such bookends, the beginning containing foretastes of what the end will look like.**

It is not surprising that the entire Bible—human history itself—would have such bookends, the beginning containing foretastes of what the end will look like. Consider this description of the Garden of Eden:

> Now the LORD God had planted a garden in the east, in Eden; and there he put the man he had formed. And the LORD God made all kinds of trees grow out of the ground—trees that were pleasing to the eye and good for food. In the middle of the garden were the tree of life and the tree of the knowledge of good and evil. A river watering the garden flowed from Eden ... Then the man and his wife heard the sound of the LORD God as He was walking in the garden. (Genesis 2:8-10, 3:8)

Notice three things in this account: a river, trees, and God's presence.

That was the beginning of the Bible. Now look at the very last chapter, when the city of God will come upon the earth:

> Then the angel showed me the river of the water of life, as clear as crystal, flowing from the throne of God and of the Lamb down the middle of the great street of the city. On each side of the river stood the tree of life, bearing twelve crops of fruit, yielding its fruit every month. And the leaves of the tree are for the healing of the nations. . . . There will be no more night. They will not need the light of a lamp or the light of the sun, for the Lord God will give them light. And they will reign for ever and ever. (Revelation 22:1-2, 5)

Again we have a river, trees, and God's presence. Bookends for human history and for the Bible itself.

Interestingly, there is one more account in the middle of the Bible with the same details. This describes the outpouring of the Holy Spirit, in our days and in days to come.

> The man brought me back to the entrance of the temple, and I saw water coming out from under the threshold of the temple toward the east (for the temple faced east). The water was coming down from under the south side of the temple, south of the altar. . . . As the man went eastward with a measuring line in his hand, he measured off a thousand cubits and then led me through water that was ankle-deep. He measured off another thousand cubits and led me through water that was knee-deep. He measured off another thousand and led me through water that was up to the waist. He measured off another thousand, but now it was a river that I could not cross, because the water had risen and was deep enough to swim in—a river that no one could cross. He asked me,

> "Son of man, do you see this?" Then he led me back to the bank of the river. When I arrived there, I saw a great number of trees on each side of the river. . . . Fruit trees of all kinds will grow on both banks of the river. Their leaves will not wither, nor will their fruit fail. Every month they will bear, because the water from the sanctuary flows to them. Their fruit will serve for food and their leaves for healing." (Ezekiel 47:1, 3-7, 12)

Again we have a river, trees, and God's presence. The similarity with the other verses shows that this outpouring can be thought of as heaven experienced on the earth. It is a description of the ministry of the Kingdom, both in Jesus' day and in ours. This is the doing of the Alpha and the Omega, simultaneously the beginning, the end, and the in-between! And He is giving it to us to taste it even now.

The Kingdom of God

The Kingdom of God (or Kingdom of heaven) is mentioned over 100 times in the New Testament. It is God's rule and reign. Jesus' words described the Kingdom; His works demonstrated it. Just as the kingdom of the enemy is characterized by darkness, deceit, disease, destruction, bondage, and death, the Kingdom of God is characterized by light, truth, healing, growth, freedom, and life. When Jesus came, He brought the Kingdom as a heavenly invasion, obliterating the kingdom of darkness wherever the two collided. Disease was replaced by healing, bondage by freedom, and death by life.

Some might ask, was this Kingdom Jesus spoke of now or in the future? Some verses speak of it as being now: "Heal the sick who are there and tell them, 'The kingdom of God is near you.'" (Luke 10:9). Others speak of it as coming in the future: "I say to you that many will come from the east and the west, and will take their places at the feast with Abraham,

Isaac and Jacob in the kingdom of heaven." (Matthew 8:11). Therefore, as George Eldon Ladd often said, it is both now and not yet!

The ministry of Jesus, therefore, can be thought of as the future invading the now—where foreshocks of the not-yet are made manifest in the now. Jesus, the Alpha and the Omega, was calling upon the Omega (heaven) to be manifest now.

> **The ministry of Jesus can be thought of as the future invading the now – where foreshocks of the not-yet are made manifest in the now.**

When His disciples asked Jesus to teach them to pray the way He prayed, He said, "Let Your Kingdom come, let Your will be done on earth as it is in heaven." This describes His own desire and ministry, that the future Kingdom be demonstrated here and now. He was asking us to pray this into being—that the not-yet invade the now. In other words, we are praying that the river of heaven flow down the streets of the earth.

This is what Ezekiel 47 is portraying: the flow of God's Spirit bringing in His Kingdom, pictured as heaven pouring onto the earth. (Note: It is interesting to compare this with John 7:38 where Jesus speaks of rivers of living water.) Although the fullness of heaven will come on the Last Day, this is a foretaste and foreshock of it. This was Jesus' ministry, and He wants us to experience the same flow of the Kingdom in our day to show the reality and goodness of His reign.

Bringers of the Not-Yet

When Jesus was on earth, *He* led the heavenly invasion of God's Kingdom. Now He has asked *us* to be the precipitators of the Kingdom of God. The Lord's Prayer is what He gave *us* to pray. In it, He is giving *us* the mandate and authority to pray that the Kingdom break into our world.

> **He is giving us the mandate and authority to pray that the Kingdom break into our world.**

The phrases, "Let Your Kingdom come, let Your will be done on earth as it is in heaven" are actually in the imperative tense, as if we are speaking those things to be done: "Kingdom, come! Will as in heaven, be done!" We are ordained, as if priests or ambassadors, to speak these to the world. We are carriers of God's authority to call the not-yet to come into the now. This is who we are.

To see what this looks like, look at the ministry of Jesus or of any of the disciples. They were callers of the Kingdom. However their lives were not always easy and they carried humble, giving, tenacious, sacrificial hearts. This combination—of the power of the Kingdom and hearts like these—touched the world, often confounding the wise, but such were the ones God loved to use to display His amazing Kingdom. So, too, God will use us.

As this chapter began, we explored a fascinating aspect of God's character: His timelessness. It is not surprising that it characterized the ministry of Jesus. But it is overwhelming, yet true, that Jesus called us to this very same ministry. And it is the same not-yet-and-now characteristic that He is calling us to employ in order to bring His Kingdom to the earth. He is calling us to be "Bringers of the Not Yet"—bringers of the future light, truth, healing, freedom, and life that are part of heaven's Kingdom to the earth today.

Looking Forward

What I have shared so far is a lot to digest. What does this mean for us personally? How do we walk this out? How do we live in the now and also in the not-yet? To walk in the now and the not-yet, our gaze has to be forward. As Paul told the Philippians:

> One thing I do: Forgetting what is behind and straining toward what is ahead, I press on toward the goal to win the prize for which God has called me heavenward in Christ Jesus. (Philippians 3:13b-14)

Before I say what I mean by this, let me say what I don't mean. First, I don't mean that we shouldn't look backwards to the cross and all that it accomplished. The cross is essential to keep our life centered. Even though it happened in the past, it is one of those timeless things that overarches all we are and ever will be. Second, I don't mean that we should simply ignore our hurts of the past and not seek healing for them. Sweeping them under the rug will keep us in our hurts and prevent us from going forward. God wants to heal us so that we can fully look forward. Third, I don't mean that we should ignore the past without having reflected upon it to better our character. We need to use it to show us how we need to change. Having done this, however, we must not dwell there, but we must go forward—our gaze must not dwell on the past nor on ourselves. We must look forward, seeing the future God has destined for us.

> **Our looking heavenward, on the not-yet, gives us focus, confidence and direction.**

If you have ever tried to walk or drive a car by only looking where you have been, you are going to travel in some pretty strange directions! Looking forward gives us stability and a sense of direction. If you look at people that the world admires, they usually have a sense of confidence or direction. Often movie stars have this persona (although many may be coached in how to have this image). How often do we, however, try to go forward yet end up looking behind, our hands flailing away at memories of the past, entangled in thoughts of how we have fallen short, sinned, or been victimized? No wonder it is hard to go forward. Paul speaks to this very thing:

> Therefore I do not run like a man running aimlessly; I do not fight like a man beating the air. (1 Corinthians 9:26)

Paul is comparing our life in the Lord with that of an athlete, whose focus is forward upon the prize. He speaks of the training they go through, with a focus on where they are heading. So, too, our looking heavenward—on the not-yet—gives us such focus, confidence, and direction. And when we are looking at the not-yet, we know one of our calls is to bring that not-yet into the now.

Citizens of the Not-Yet

As we become dual citizens of the not-yet and the now, we are sanctioned to call the not-yet into the now. We are authorized to bring the Kingdom of God to the world, offering healing, freedom, and newness of life. Empowered with authority—like prophets with their staffs in their hands—we thrust our staffs into the ground saying, "Kingdom of God, come!" and then watch as His Kingdom bursts onto the scene. This is who we are called to be.

3
Who Are You?

One morning as I was lying in bed, I got another piece of the puzzle. I felt the Lord telling me to consider the story of the sons of Sceva.

> Some Jews who went around driving out evil spirits tried to invoke the name of the Lord Jesus over those who were demon-possessed. They would say, "In the name of Jesus, whom Paul preaches, I command you to come out." Seven sons of Sceva, a Jewish chief priest, were doing this. One day the evil spirit answered them, "Jesus I know, and I know about Paul, but who are you?" Then the man who had the evil spirit jumped on them and overpowered them all. He gave them such a beating that they ran out of the house naked and bleeding. (Acts 19:13-16)

The Lord posed a question in my mind: How do you apply this to your life? My first thought was that most people would say, "Those sons of Sceva were crazy. I would never do *that*!" I instantly felt, however, that this was not the answer God was looking for. In Mark 9:38-41, when the disciples saw someone who was not a disciple driving out demons, Jesus told them not to stop him, for "whoever is not against us is for us."

I felt the Lord say, "What I'm looking for is that you must be able to answer, 'Who are you?'" That was the important question. Of course, the sons of Sceva, who were not in a relationship with Jesus, had no satisfactory answer to this and were left overpowered by the evil one. But we who are in a relationship with Jesus need to be able to answer this question as well. That way *we* can be the ones who do the overpowering.

> Like the lion son in the movie *Lion King*, we already have an identity but will not be able to do anything effectively until we realize what that identity is.

What I am talking about is knowing our own identity. Like the lion son in the movie *Lion King*, we already have an identity but will not be able to do anything effectively until we realize what that identity is.

As I lay in bed thinking about all this, I knew the Lord had, for a while, been talking to my wife about identity, too. So I decided to ask her as she was waking up, "Who are you?" In retrospect, I realize that this is not the best thing to say to your wife first thing in the morning. (Don't try this at home!) But she actually understood what I was saying and took it as one more nudge from the Lord to know who she is.

The Importance of Our Identity

Some may be agreeing wholeheartedly with the importance of knowing who we are. Others may be thinking of some objections. I can think of several objections they might have.

One objection might be that it is not important to know who *we* are; it is important to know who *God* is. I agree with the second half of this. It is vitally important to know who God is. Only through knowing this can we know who we are in Him. But to know who we are is important, too. I will point out the numerous Scriptures which show how intently God wants us to know who we now are. The story of our redemption involves us being changed into something new. We need to know what that "something new" is—how God sees us—and how this propels us into doing what He has called us to do.

A second objection might be that it was an evil spirit that asked "Who are you?" and we only care about what God thinks. Again, the second half is true. However, the evil spirit was just exploiting a weakness in the seven sons of not knowing who they were. The critical question is, does *God* want us to know who we are? I hope to show how very true and crucial this is.

Just to give you a taste of how much this is stressed in Scripture, consider two subjects: the forgiveness of sins and being made righteous. Of course, these are intimately connected. The former involves the removal of the negative (at a costly price to Jesus); the latter involves the addition of a positive. In terms of identity, sin gave us the identity of a condemned man. Forgiveness took that identity away. But being made righteous gives us the identity of one who could stand and even glow in God's presence. If a prisoner is pardoned by the president, he is no longer considered guilty and is free to go his own way. But the identity which God has given us is far beyond this—we have an identity of honor, not to mention being carriers of His presence, partners with Him in His ministry, and part of His family.

In all of his writings, Paul uses the word *forgiveness* twice. That is not to take one thing away from how astonishingly important this truth is. However, he uses the word *righteous* fifty five times! It is clear that God, through Paul, wants to establish our identity.

Another objection might be that knowing our amazing identity somehow competes with our efforts toward humility, embracing the cross, and overcoming sin in our lives. These are indeed important, but knowing our identity is a boon, not a deterrent to these things. Paul speaks of these things in his letters, but only after establishing our identity of righteousness in God. Our identity is a grace that empowers us to live the way we are supposed to live. Someone might say, too, that spending time to know our identity is a self-centered exercise. The truth is, dwelling in the false identity which the world and the enemy has given us keeps us constantly focused upon ourselves. The identity which God has given us brings us the freedom of not having to pump up our own self-worth. We are free of ourselves, free to place ourselves in God's hands, free to look only to Him, and free to serve others.

> **Who we are in the Lord is light years beyond anything else.**

There is more to the importance of knowing who we are. There are voices in the secular world that have risen to a high degree of popularity because they tell people, "You are somebody." I won't take that away from them. The truth is, however, that who we are in the Lord is light years beyond any of this. It can stagger our minds. But our minds need to be staggered in this way if we are to fulfill what God has called us to: working in a world of darkness and bringing in His marvelous light. The world offers no position, honor, or profession higher (or more stable) than who we are in the Lord.

Knowing who we are is extremely important. As the passage about the sons of Sceva shows, without it, we can be thrown around by the enemy. With it, we can maintain a steady and powerful course in doing what God has called us to do. My friend George Koch, a remarkable pastor in the Anglican Church, once had a dream in which a huge demonic figure was inflicting fear on the church. The figure grabbed George by the collar and lifted him off his feet, bringing them together face to face. It said, "What's your name?" Struck by terror, George's mind went blank, but then he heard himself saying, "I am a servant of the Lord washed by His blood." At that the figure pushed George away. The world and the enemy are out to control us by fear and manipulation. Jesus has an answer to that, and part of that answer lies in establishing our identity in Him. With it, we are free from being manhandled by the enemy or anyone else who would try to stop us from knowing and serving the Lord.

4
Authority

The last chapter spoke of the undesirable consequences of trying to move in authority without a grounding in identity. To establish the connection between authority and identity, let me give a brief background on authority.

In prayer ministry, especially in ministering healing, there are many different types of prayer: intercession, petition, and the like. However, in studying the prayers of Jesus as He ministered healing, we find a somewhat surprising approach. His prayers were extremely short! Often He commanded parts of the body to work (such as "See!"). Other times, He seemed to skip prayer (as we know it) all together and just tell the person to do something their condition would not have allowed them to do (such as "Take up your mat and walk."). It was clear that in doing these things, He was moving in authority. Authority is what we need to understand. It is something God is highlighting today.

The Greek word for authority is *exousia*. *Exousia* is like the badge of a policeman. It is probably the police officer's most effective device for being obeyed. We know that if we should choose to disobey, he could bring the entire force of the city, state, or nation down upon us.

Or consider a soldier. Even armed with the most sophisticated weapons, if you, as a soldier, went into the enemy's camp, walked up to the commander and demanded he surrender, he would probably laugh in your face because there would be one of you compared to his thousands. If, on the other hand, he were to look over your shoulder and see an army of millions behind you, and you were speaking in the authority of that army, your words would carry a lot of weight. So authority—*exousia*, can be very effective.

> **The authority we use in ministry is delegated authority. It comes from who Jesus says we are and whom we represent.**

The authority we use in ministry is *delegated* authority. It comes from who Jesus says we are and whom we represent. Jesus used authority. When He spoke, everybody knew He had it. He also delegated authority to His disciples and showed them how it worked (Luke 9:1). And, as we shall see, He teaches us the amazing fact that we, too, have authority and shows us how to use it.

Authority and Relationship

To be *in* authority, we must be *under* authority. Jesus was an example of this. Even though, being God, Jesus could have had authority in and of Himself, it says in Philippians 2 that He became a servant and walked under the authority of His Father. He said, "I only do what I see the Father doing." (John 5:19). He modeled how we are to walk. Walking in the Father's authority went hand in hand with being in continual relationship with His Father. At the very beginning of Jesus' ministry, when He was baptized by John the Baptist, the Father spoke from heaven, saying, "You are My Son . . ." Relationship was central in Jesus' authority and ministry and must be so in ours.

History of our Authority in God

One might ask, "If God is sovereign, does anything we do really make a difference?" In other words, what is our authority doing if God's will is going to be done regardless of what we do? God certainly is sovereign, but in His sovereignty He has ordained that what we say and do can affect the course of human history. In His sovereignty, He has chosen to give us authority.

In Genesis 1 we see that the subduing of the earth was an authority that He had given to man.

> Then God said, "Let us make man in our image, in our likeness, and let them rule over the fish of the sea and the birds of the air, over the livestock, over all the earth, and over all the creatures that move along the ground." So God created man in his own image; in the image of God he created him; male and female he created them. God blessed them, and said, "Be fruitful and increase in number; fill the earth and subdue it. Rule over the fish of the sea and the birds of the air and over every living creature that moves on the ground." (Genesis 1:26-28)

Psalm 8 and 115 reiterate this.

> You made [man] a little lower than the heavenly beings and crowned him with glory and honor. You made him ruler over the works of your hands; you put everything under his feet: all flocks and herds, and the beasts of the field, the birds of the air, and the fish of the sea, all that swim the paths of the seas. (Psalm 8:5-8)

> The highest heavens belong to the Lord, but the earth He has given to man. (Psalm 115:16)

Luke adds a new twist to this issue. When Jesus was tempted in the wilderness, we are told:

> The devil led him up to a high place and showed him in an instant all the kingdoms of the world. And he said to him, "I will give you all their authority and splendor, for it has been given to me, and I can give it to anyone I want to. So if you worship me, it will all be yours."
>
> Jesus answered, "It is written: 'Worship the Lord your God and serve him only.'" (Luke 4:5-8)

Notice that Jesus did not argue whether Satan's words were true—the authority God had given to us had, at least in part, been given over to Satan through our sin in the Garden of Eden. If this had no element of truth, then the temptation would have been empty. To some extent we had lost our authority.

That's not the end of the story about authority, thankfully. After Jesus' death and resurrection, Matthew 28 states,

> Then Jesus came to them and said, "All authority in heaven and on earth has been given to me. Therefore go and make disciples of all nations . . ." (Matthew 28:18)

Jesus won back this authority by His death on the cross. He took the keys from Satan. When Jesus tells us, "All authority has been given to Me on heaven and earth; therefore go . . ." the implication is that Jesus is giving us authority too. This authority will affect our going and what we do when we go.

In Matthew 16 Jesus said,

> "I will give you the keys of the kingdom of heaven; whatever you bind on earth will be bound in heaven, and whatever you loose on earth will be loosed in heaven." (Matthew 16:19)

Again He is saying that He is giving us authority. We now have the keys, a symbol of authority and the openers of every gate. This is reminiscent of Isaiah's words:

> "I will . . . hand your authority over to him . . . I will place on his shoulder the key to the house of David; what he opens no one can shut, and what he shuts no one can open." (Isaiah 22:21-23)

> **The authority is ours: from opening the gates of heaven to closing the gates of destruction over a person's life.**

When Scripture uses opposites, such as binding vs. loosing or opening vs. shutting, it is speaking of something that is all inclusive. The authority is ours: from opening the gates of heaven to closing the gates of destruction over a person's life. The power to separate (for example, a person and their sickness) or bring together (a person and God) is very inclusive in all that we do.

Jesus also says we have the authority to separate a man from his sins: "If you forgive anyone his sins, they are forgiven; if you do not forgive them, they are not forgiven." (John 20:23). Even the Pharisees were astonished at this, "Who can forgive sins but God alone?" (Luke 5:21). But that authority, too, He has delegated to His people.

Another way He tells us He has given us authority is His invitation to pray in His name. This concept is similar to that of exercising power of attorney. We can write a check signing His name. Whatever we ask or say will be taken by the Father as if Jesus were asking or saying it Himself.

God is indeed sovereign, but He has chosen to give us authority and, therefore, will act in response to our words and actions. Remember, however, that this is all in the context of our relationship with Him. We live in a place where His heart beats within our heart, His will becomes our will.

God's Will Expressed in Our Words

There is something about God in that He likes to speak before He acts. In creation, the word was spoken and then He acted—"Let there be light," and there was light (Genesis 1:3). Having come into His Kingdom through redemption in His Son, God has purposed to bring us into an amazing partnership with Him as His ministry continues and His Kingdom spreads. One of the ways this partnership works is that He asks *us* to be the one speaking His words before He moves. God shows us His will which then needs to be expressed in words. In His sovereignty, that's what He is looking for us to do.

> **One of the ways this partnership works is that He asks us to be the one speaking His words before He moves.**

Of course, we don't have to figure out every aspect of God's will before we can do this. Like David, we are constantly communicating with Him, friend to friend. In the process, God allows His heart to be felt in ours. This needs to be expressed in words, whether in petition or prayer of command. God, then, moves in response to what we ask or say. That we are a part of this process is staggeringly awesome—but it is imperative that we know how it works.

In Daniel 10:12, the angel Gabriel was sent in response to Daniel's prayer. Gabriel said, "Your words were heard and I have come in response to them." Daniel's prayer was followed by God's action.

In James 5 we see:

> The prayer of a righteous man is powerful and effective. Elijah was a man just like us. He prayed earnestly that it would not rain, and it did not rain on the land for three and a half years. Again he prayed, and the heavens gave rain, and the earth produced its crops. (James 5:16b-18)

Elijah expressed the will of the Lord in words and God acted. James asserts that we are just like Elijah; the things we ask in prayer the Lord will do.

Jesus taught His disciples to say: "Your will be done on earth as it is in heaven." (Matthew 6:10). He is saying that we are to express in words the desire that the Father's will be done. This expression is a necessary step in the process of God's will being done on earth. The sovereign God has made it so.

Prayers of Command

Prayers of command, like those short prayers of Jesus, are directed at whatever needs to be changed. We are not commanding God! Rather, we are expressing His will. Unlike the concept of prayer being directed toward God, this is directed from Him, or on behalf of Him, such as speaking to parts of the body to be healed or pain to go. This brings up an interesting question: are these commands prophetic expressions of what He is saying to us at the time, or are they our words based on a general knowledge of what He wants to be done? The answer is both. Like a police chief and his officers, He has given us authority to bring the Kingdom. We don't need to constantly ask the chief what to do when we see a criminal robbing a store. We just intervene. However, unlike this analogy of a policeman and his chief, we are filled with God's presence and are constantly in tune with His voice and heart, accessible to His telling us the best way to approach each situation. So we have both a general sense of the ways of the King burning within us, and also hearts and ears receptive to His heart and voice, delighted with what we sense and hear from Him so that others are empowered and set free.

Authority and Identity

Clearly, to use the authority God wants us to use, we need to know that we have it. And this is connected with knowing who we are. Those who carry the world's authority: policemen, military officers, mayors, presidents, and kings, also carry the identity associated with their roles. Without truly knowing their identity they could not exercise their authority in the way it should be exercised—they would either ignore the responsibility that comes with their identity and fail to use their authority to bring about change, or they would operate with a sense of insecurity, which can greatly damage the way authority is used. The world has known too many leaders that have failed in these ways.

> **To use authority well, we have to know who we are.**

To use authority well, we have to know who we are. Then it will become second nature for us to use it, displaying the heart of God as we help those in need of His intervention. As this comes into place, we are poised to change our corner of the world.

5
Identity

God, throughout the Old and New Testaments, clearly felt identity was important. In Scripture, *names*, particularly the names given by God, were well thought out to encapsulate a person's identity. Throughout history, God revealed who He was and connected those revelations with names for Himself to show us His own identity. There was *Yahweh*, with the profound meaning, "I Am." When He spoke of and demonstrated His desire to heal, he called Himself *Yahweh Rapha*, meaning "God who heals." With His desire to provide, He called Himself *Yahweh Yireh*, "God who provides." He also is God-our-Righteousness (*Yahweh Tsadeq*), God-of-Armies (*Yahweh Sabaoth*), and God-who-is-Mighty (*El Shaddai*).

Jesus continued this practice, giving Himself many different names, each describing a different aspect of His identity. In the book of John, there are seven major discourses, each with different "I Am" names describing who He is (*I am the Good Shepherd, I am the Bread of Life*, etc.). And finally in the book of John, when the troops came asking who He was in order to arrest Him, He simply stated, "I AM." And the soldiers fell over at the sheer power of these words.

Focusing on our New Identities

Another piece of the puzzle in my realizing the importance of who we are came in the person of Todd White. Todd is a very likeable, amazing person, well known for bringing healing and prophetic words to the streets. His looks, with his dreadlocks and laid-back attire, sets him entirely under the radar of people on the lookout for religiosity. Hearing he was coming to a local church, Mary and I were eager to attend. He was doing a two-day training seminar on ministering in the streets. I was very interested to see how he taught on healing and prophetic ministry, since I like those subjects too. To my surprise, however, he spent the entire first evening talking about how we are the righteousness of God. I found that curious, although I enjoyed the evening immensely. I found myself feeling lighter and full of energy afterwards, and that night had dreams of flying and riding motorcycles.

In pondering why Todd had started this way, I could see how much more ready I was to go out and do the ministry of God. I could see how focusing on our identity in the Lord was key in everything we do. It teaches us how to walk. And how we see ourselves is what we become.

> **How we see ourselves is what we become.**

Hooking this into the other pieces of the puzzle God had been revealing in prior months—our authority and our identity as bringers of the not-yet into the now—started changing the way I saw things and the way I saw myself. It put a new spring into my steps. In my walks around our neighborhood, I realized how God had given me everything His righteousness gives us access to, and how I truly was a Kingdom-caller and light-bearer. I felt an inner readiness to call in the Kingdom whenever the occasion arose, and I called it in prophetically, whether interceding for households or speaking to someone, for I knew I had the authority and mandate to do so.

This made such a difference in the way I felt and saw things day by day. Was there a battle to stay in this awareness? Very much so! But if I battled my way there in the morning, it made an incredible difference the rest of the day. I saw, too, the importance of continuously speaking the truth of who we

Identity

are to each other. The world and the enemy do their best to drain this away. But with it, God's people can come alive.

The Cost of Having Negative Identities

One of the ways the enemy and the world can suppress the Body of Christ is to chip away at our identities in the Lord, replacing them with false and destructive substitutes. It grieves me to see this, and I know it does God too. These negative identities can include recurring thoughts such as, "I am a failure," "I am worthless," "I am stupid," "I will never amount to anything," "I am rejected," "I am unlovable," "I am an outsider and can never have friends," "I am beyond help," "God cannot use me," and the like.

These types of identities come from fears. Sometimes they can bring the reality of what we fear into our lives. The fear of failure can produce failure by making us lack the confidence to try new things, follow our dreams, or press through to success. The fear of rejection can sometimes be subconsciously perceived and agreed with by others (often with the enemy's help). However, in the Lord we can demolish these fears and stop their destructive spiral. (Note: Besides the fear-based identities I am covering here, other things can attempt to label us, such as when we are victimized by circumstances. We must not let circumstances define who we are, however. Our identity is in God's hands.)

> **These destructive fears and identities have many costs.**

These destructive fears and identities have many costs. They can take us off the track of what is best to do. For example, when King Saul failed to do what God desired, he spoke of his fear of people, "I have sinned. I violated the

LORD's command and your instructions. I was afraid of the people and so I gave in to them." (1 Samuel 15: 24).

Such identities can also trap us in a spirit of poverty, in isolation, or in a downward life style. Identities laced with insecurities can cause us to waste time and energy trying to figure out what others think of us (fearing they will think the worst) or ways to impress them.

These identities can be exploited by the enemy and others. If we fear rejection, others can manipulate us by hinting they will reject us if we do not do their bidding, or by getting us emotionally dependent on their approval so we do what they want. They sense we will do anything to avoid what we fear.

Some people react to this manipulation by getting down on themselves. Others prevent being manipulated by trying to manipulate others first. Or they may reject others before they are rejected first, or criticize others before they are criticized first. When we are in this place, one word meant as a suggestion can be interpreted as an attack against our identity, sending us into a tailspin and ruining our self-worth. The feeling of being controlled by people in this way can have further negative consequences. It can lead to anger and resentment in us. Or it can result in our withdrawing from and avoiding people. It can often spur jealousy by comparing ourselves with what other people have. And all of this can lead to depression, worry, people-pleasing, or people-mashing. But God can change all that.

If, in the past, authority figures have damaged our identity, we may now seek approval or boosts to our identity through other authority figures in an unhealthy way. However, we may retain a conscious or unconscious fear of being shot down and are overly defensive to them. This stands in the way with what could be a productive relationship with those in authority.

Fears and negative identities can also take away from the influence of the Holy Spirit. We won't attempt the dreams God has given. It can also lead us down the path of thinking

Identity

that we have to earn God's acceptance by what we do, not believing that He loves and accepts us by a gift of His grace.

> **When we hand our identity and sense of approval over to Him, we are free indeed.**

Through these fears and negative identities, we are giving our source of approval and identity (what we base our self-worth upon) to someone else that rightfully belongs to God. We can become addicted to getting this approval elsewhere. But God is jealous that these things belong to Him. When we hand our identity and sense of approval over to Him, we are free indeed.

Some Causes of Negative Identities

Not surprisingly, Satan has set out to rob us of the joy of the identity we have in God. Sometimes he places fears within us in order to replace our identity with a destructive one, and he tries to make us latch onto those fears. Sometimes those fears have their roots in our experiences with authority figures, sometimes even from a very early age. These authority figures could be fathers, mothers, teachers, churches, or teachings. They can affect both our identity and the way we view God.

For the purpose of illustration, let me highlight how our experience with our own father can affect us. Please note that some of us were blessed to have very caring fathers. Others had fathers that simply never knew what it was to be loved and therefore it was difficult to know how to show love.

- With an ***abusive father*** (verbally or mentally), we just don't know when we'll get whacked. We feel we can't let our guard down. This can lead to a similar view of God, inhibiting our intimacy with Him. It can also lead to our fear of authority figures and an identity of being worthless and unlovable.

- With a ***missing or aloof father***, we can't trust that God or people will always be there for us. This can lead to an identity where we cannot believe we are worth enough that God would always be there for us.

- With a ***father who manipulates by guilt and fear of punishment***, we think that this is the way things are. We can't imagine how God would guide our behavior any differently. We can't imagine looking in God's eyes and seeing favor, but rather seeing how we have fallen short in something. This leads to an identity where we are afraid of failure, thinking we will never amount to anything, or looking at ourselves as unlikeable.

- With a ***father whom we can never please***, we never can quite fit into his mold. So we think God is never pleased. This leads to an identity of thinking no one can ever be completely pleased with us.

- With an ***inexpressive father***, we rarely or never heard that he loved or appreciated us. So we became resigned to the fact this will never happen. We may even believe we are not lovable or have nothing anyone could appreciate.

> **These affect both our identity as well as the identity of God in our lives.**

Note how these affect our own identity as well as the identity of God in our lives. This is just one thing that can block us from enjoying God. (No wonder the enemy is trying to break apart families.) That is why Jesus spent so much time talking about what God the Father is like. And, in so doing, our own identities are recreated.

Of course, there are many other negative experiences that can lead to damaged identities. Teachers can speak bleak words about our abilities and future. Pastors can paint inaccurate pictures of God and where we stand with Him. Spouses can speak hurtful words about our characters and ability to love. Friends and coworkers can stab us with painful words and insinuations. But God has amazing things to say to us. And whose words can compare with His—He who created us and gave us life?

The Remedy for a Negative Identity

Fortunately, whatever negative identity the enemy is trying to place upon us, the Lord can shatter it through the remarkable truth of what our identity really is. Here are some ways to shatter the old identities and wear the new.

- Ask God to help. He is jealous for you and His heartfelt desire is to help you in this. He is the truth and the truth will set you free.

- Discover what your false identity is. God will help you see what it is and where it came from.

- Slay this false identity with the Sword of the Spirit and replace it with what God thinks. Find the true identity the Lord has given you (ask someone for ministry if you don't know what it is) and write it down. Read it every day. That is truth and it will set you free.

- See things from God's perspective. He far exceeds our own understanding, even of the way we see ourselves.

- Realize that identity and approval either come from God or from man—we cannot seek both. He wants to be Lord of our life and is unwilling to share that rightful Lordship with anyone else. He alone is the final authority on who we are and on our acceptance. He deeply loves us, completely forgives us, and totally accepts us.

- The most fundamental identity we have is that we are God's very own. He smiles upon us and delights in us. We are His sons and daughters (Galatians 4:6-7). Jesus calls us His friend (John 15:15). Build your identity starting with that.

- Help others in this struggle: offer them an accepting, encouraging environment and speak into what their identity truly is.

The next chapter shows us what our true God-given identity is and the price He paid to give it to us. Having slain the old, it is time to know what God is replacing it with. Realize, too, that the enemy and the world are so intent in draining us, that we will have to, each day, look in the mirror and speak the truth of who we are to ourselves. But it is God's truth and God's word, and that word will not return void, but will be endued with the power to turn our false realities into true ones. And that will bear fruit, giving life to you and to many.

6
Jesus' Identity and Ours

As mentioned in the last chapter, the Bible shows that there was often considerable thought that went into names. There were many names given to God. And God would often change people's names, which represented the work He had done in their lives and identities. He changed *Abram* (exalted father) to *Abraham* (the father of many), *Jacob* (heal-grabber) to *Israel* (wrestler with God). But we don't do that much anymore. So should names, or at least phrases depicting who we are, be important to us? Yes! Jesus has given us an amazing identity. We don't have to change our surnames, but we should think of what Jesus calls us when we think of ourselves.

Who Jesus Is

First, consider how many names were given to Jesus establishing His identity. The list is immense.

Advocate (1 John 2:1)
Almighty (Rev. 1:8)
Alpha and Omega (Rev. 1:8; 22:13)
Amen (Rev. 3:14)
Apostle and High Priest (Heb. 3:1)
Atoning Sacrifice (1 John 2:2)
Author and Perfecter of our Faith (Heb. 12:2)
Author of Life (Acts 3:15)

Author of Our Salvation (Heb. 2:10)
Beginning and End (Rev. 22:13)
Blessed and only Ruler (1 Tim. 6:15)
Bread of Life (John 6:35; 6:48)
Bridegroom (Matt. 9:15)
Capstone (Acts 4:11; 1 Pet. 2:7)
Chief Cornerstone (Eph. 2:20)
Chief Shepherd (1 Pet. 5:4)
Deliverer (Rom. 11:26)
Eternal Life (1 John 1:2; 5:20)
Everlasting Father (Isa. 9:6)
Faithful and True (Rev. 19:11)
Faithful and True Witness (Rev. 3:14)
Faithful Witness (Rev. 1:5)
First and Last (Rev. 1:17; 2:8; 22:13)
Firstborn from the dead (Rev. 1:5)
Firstborn over all creation (Col. 1:15)
Gate for the Sheep (John 10:7)
God (John 1:1; 20:28; Heb. 1:8; Rom. 9:5)
Good Shepherd (John 10:11,14)
Great Shepherd of the Sheep (Heb. 13:20)
Great High Priest (Heb. 4:14)
Head of the Church (Eph. 1:22; 4:15; 5:23)
Heir of all things (Heb. 1:2)
High Priest (Heb. 5:10)
Holy and True (Rev. 3:7)
Holy and Righteous One (Acts 3:14)
Hope (1 Tim. 1:1)
Hope of Glory (Col. 1:27)
Horn of Salvation (Luke 1:69)
I Am (John 8:58)
Image of God (2 Cor. 4:4)
Immanuel (*God with Us*) (Matt. 1:23)
Jesus (*God who Saves*) (Matt. 1:21, Luke 1:31)
Judge of the living and the dead (Acts 10:42)
King (Matt. 21:5)
King Eternal (1 Tim. 1:17)
King of Israel (John 1:49)

King of the Jews (Matt. 2:2)
King of kings (1 Tim. 6:15; Rev. 19:16)
King of the Ages (Rev. 15:3)
Lamb (Rev. 13:8, 15:3)
Lamb of God (John 1:29)
Lamb without Blemish (1 Pet. 1:19)
Last Adam (1 Cor. 15:45)
Light of the World (John 8:12)
Lion of the Tribe of Judah (Rev. 5:5)
Living One (Rev. 1:18)
Living Stone (1 Pet. 2:4)
Lord (Matt. 21:3; 2 Pet. 2:20)
Lord of All (Acts 10:36)
Lord of Glory (1 Cor. 2:8)
Lord of lords (1 Tim. 6:15; Rev. 19:16)
Lord of the Sabbath (Matt. 12:8)
Man from Heaven (1 Cor. 15:48)
Mediator between God and Man (1 Tim. 2:5)
Mediator of the New Covenant (Heb. 9:15)
Messiah (Christ) (Matt. 1:16; 16:16)
Mighty God (Isa. 9:6)
Morning Star (Rev. 22:16)
Only Begotten Son of God (John 1:18; 1 John 4:9)
Only Wise God (1 Tim. 1:17)
Our Great God and Savior (Titus 2:13)
Our Holiness (1 Cor. 1:30)
Our Husband (2 Cor. 11:2)
Our Passover Lamb (1 Cor. 5:7)
Our Redemption (1 Cor. 1:30)
Our Righteousness (1 Cor. 1:30)
Power of God (1 Cor. 1:24)
Precious Cornerstone (1 Pet. 2:6)
Prince of Peace (Isa. 9:6)
Prophet (Luke 13:33)
Resurrection and the Life (John 11:25)
Righteous Branch (Jer. 23:5)
Righteous One (Acts 7:52; 1 John 2:1)
Rock (1 Cor. 10:4)

Root and Offspring of David (Rev. 5:5; 22:16)
Ruler of God's Creation (Rev. 3:14)
Ruler of the Kings of the Earth (Rev. 1:5)
Savior (Luke 2:11; Eph. 5:23; Titus 1:4; 2 Pet. 2:20)
Servant (Matt. 12:18)
Son of Abraham (Matt. 1:1)
Son of David (Matt. 1:1)
Son of God (John 1:49; Heb. 4:14)
Son of Man (Matt.10:23, 12:8)
Son of the Living God (Matt. 16:16)
Son of the Most High God (Luke 1:32)
Source of Eternal Salvation (Heb. 5:9)
Stone the builders rejected (Acts 4:11)
Teacher (*Rabbi*) (Matt. 23:8; John 1:49)
The Way, the Truth and the Life (John 14:6)
True Bread (John 6:32)
True God (John 17:3, 1 John 2:20)
True Light (John 1:9)
True Vine (John 15:1)
Wisdom of God (1 Cor. 1:24)
Wonderful Counselor (Isa. 9:6)
Word (*Logos*) (John 1:1)
Word of God (Rev. 19:13)
Your Life (Col. 3:4)

The Great Exchange

As this list (which is a partial one at that) shows, Jesus had a wondrous identity. As the sacrificial Lamb of God, however, He did something astounding on our behalf. What took place at His death upon the cross is what I call the *Great Exchange*. On the cross, what we deserved was given to Him; what He deserved was given to us. He was sinless and deserved a crown of righteousness and everlasting life. We deserved shame and death. He, however, took on our sin and experienced our shame and death. In doing so, He won for us righteousness and everlasting life. (For an interesting look at the language of exchange in the Old Testament, see Isaiah 61:3,7—a portion of a prophecy which Jesus said He came to fulfill.)

When you think about it, part of what was exchanged was identity. Paul writes in 2 Corinthians 5:21, "God made him who had no sin to be sin for us, so that in him we might become the righteousness of God." As we think of the beautiful identity He had, it is almost unthinkable that our own sin should mar this one of beauty. But the Bible goes beyond this to something almost incomprehensible—it says He *became* sin. On the cross, that became His identity. Isaiah foretold this:

> He was despised and rejected by men, a man of sorrows, and familiar with suffering. Like one from whom men hide their faces he was despised, and we esteemed him not. (Isaiah 53:3)

The sin-identity had an even greater effect on Jesus, however. 1 John 1:5 says there is no darkness in God at all. God and sin simply do not mix. So when Jesus became sin, God the Father had to turn away. He had to listen to His Son cry out at His greatest time of need: "My God, my God, why have you forsaken me?" (Matthew 27:46). The physical aspect of Jesus' death was terrifying, but the spiritual suffering, this separation from his Father whom he had always loved and known, must have been even more so.

If you ever wonder if God loves you, look at this. The extent of His suffering is the extent of His love for us. He did it because He loves us—so, so much. The exchange brought us forgiveness. It brought us life. We obtain it by telling Him that is what we want—we want Him (Romans 10:13). In doing so, our lives will never be the same again. Amazingly, the exchange also brought us a new identity: Jesus' righteousness was bestowed upon us. And with that comes a plethora of astounding identities.

Who We Are

Scripture shows the amazing identities we have because of what Jesus won on the cross. As it says in 1 Peter 2:10, "Once you were not a people, but now you are the people of God." We are His! Here is a sample of what we have become.

A Chosen People (1 Pet. 2:9)
A Holy Nation (1 Pet. 2:9)
A People Belonging to God (1 Pet. 2:9)
A Royal Priesthood (1 Pet. 2:9, Rev 5:10)
Abraham's Seed (Gal. 3:29)
Alive with Christ (Eph. 2:5)
Ambassador (2 Cor. 5:20)
Aroma of Christ (2 Cor. 2:15)
Bearer of Light (Matt. 5:14)
Bearer of Peace (Phil. 4:7)
Blessed (Eph. 1:3, 1 Pet. 3:14)
Body of Christ (1 Cor. 12:27)
Called of God (2 Tim. 1:9; Rev. 17:14)
Cared for by the Good Shepherd (John 10:14)
Changed into His Image (2 Cor. 3:18)
Child of Light (Eph. 5:8)
Chosen (Col. 3:12, 1 Thess. 1:4)
Citizen of Heaven (Eph. 2:19)
Clean (John 15:3)
Complete in Him (Col 2:10)
Crucified with Christ (Gal. 2:20)
Dead to Sin (Rom. 6:2)
Declarer of God's Praises (1 Pet. 2:9)
Doer of All Things (Phil. 4:13)
Doer of Even Greater Works (John 14:12)
Faithful (3 John 1:5)
Faithful Follower (Rev. 17:14)
Filled (Matt. 5:6)
Fisher of Men (Matt. 4:19)
Forgiven (Eph. 1:7)

Free from Condemnation (Rom. 8:1)
Friend of Jesus (John 15:15)
God's Workmanship (Eph. 2:10)
Healed (1 Pet. 2:24)
Heir of the Prophets (Acts 3:25)
His Branches (John 15:5)
His Elect (Matt. 24:31, 1 Pet. 1:1)
Holy, Without Blame (Eph. 1:4)
In Christ Jesus (1 Cor. 1:30)
In Him (John 14:20)
Inheritor of the Earth (Matt. 5:5)
Inviter of the Kingdom (Matt. 6:10)
Jesus' Brother/Sister (Matt. 12:50)
Jesus' Disciple (John 8:31)
Joint Heir with Christ (Rom. 8:17)
Knower of His Voice (John 10:3-4)
Led by the Spirit (Gal. 5:18)
Light in the Lord (Eph. 5:8)
Living Epistle (2 Cor. 3:3)
Loved (Col. 3:12; 1 Thess. 1:4)
Loved as Much as God Loves Jesus (John 17:23)
Member of God's Household (Eph. 2:19)
Minister of Reconciliation (2 Cor. 5:18)
More than a Conqueror (Rom. 8:37)
Name Written in Heaven (Luke 10:20)
New Creation (2 Cor. 5:17)
Not a Slave (Gal. 4:7)
Of Christ (1 Cor. 3:23)
Part of the Kingdom of Heaven (Matt. 5:3, Rev 5:10)
Reconciled (2 Cor. 5:18)
Redeemed (Gal. 3:13)
Righteous (2 Cor. 5:21)
Rooted in Him (Col. 2:7)
Saint (Rom. 1:7)
Salt of the Earth (Matt. 5:13)
Saved (Mark 16:16)
Sealed with the Holy Spirit (Eph. 4:30)
Seated in Heavenly Places (Eph. 2:6)

Seer of God (Matt. 5:8)
Set Free (John 8:31)
Son/Daughter of God (Matt. 5:9, Gal. 4:7)
Son/Daughter of the Most High (Luke 6:35)
Standing Firm in the Lord (1 Thess. 3:8)
Strong (1 John 2:14)
Temple of God (1 Cor. 3:17)
Temple of the Holy Spirit (1 Cor. 6:19)
The Light of the World (Matt. 5:14)
Under Grace (Rom. 6:14)
Victorious (Rev. 21:7)
With Him (Matt. 28:20, Acts 4:13)
Witness of God's Things (Luke 24:48)
Worth Many Sparrows (Matt. 10:31)

I would spend time meditating on some of these names. In looking at them, however, let us not just *know* who we are, but *be* who we are. It may take a repeated confession of what Jesus calls us in order for them to sink in. So choose some of the ones you find most difficult to believe, write them down, and put them in a place which you will see every day. Then, as they sink in, experience the feeling of freedom that they bring. More good things await after that—soon we will find that we cannot help but do more and more of the things we are privileged to do. And you might just find yourself asking, "How could I have spent so much of my life missing all of this?!?"

7
The First and Second Reformations

As I pointed out in the introduction, for years I have been intrigued not only by the first reformation, but also by the idea of a second reformation where ministry will come into the people's hands. As much as I have been longing to see this, for some reason it still has not caught on in a major way. But that may be changing.

The Second Reformation

Many have spoken of another reformation. John Stott said it well in his commentary on Ephesians:

> If the sixteenth century recovered the "priesthood of all believers" (every Christian enjoying through Christ a direct access to God), perhaps the twentieth century will recover the "ministry of all believers" (every Christian receiving from Christ a privileged ministry to men). (*The Message of Ephesians*, p.168)

This passage was part of his commentary on these verses in Ephesians 4:

> And He Himself gave some to be apostles, some prophets, some evangelists, and some pastors and teachers, for the equipping of the saints for the work of ministry, for the edifying of the body of Christ. (Ephesians 4:11-12, NKJV)

The expectation expressed in these verses is that we *all* do the work of ministry. God desires to use a variety of people, representing a variety of gifts, to equip His church for ministry (and we, in turn, may be called to equip others). As John Stott and others have said, this is so transformational that we need a reformation to bring it about. But what has stopped this reformation from catching on all these years?

When I began having a new appreciation for identity—knowing who we are—it began to hit me that this was a missing key in seeing people begin to minister with God. If, deep down, we really don't know who we are, both with regard to our access to God and to the role He has called us to play in His ministry on the earth, we may believe that He wants to use *some* people to do His works, but it is hard to believe that He wants to use *us*. Therefore it often seems more humble and less controversial just to go with the status quo and let those who have been ministering be the only ones who minister.

> **If, deep down, we really don't know who we are, we may believe that He wants to use *some* people to do His works, but it is hard to believe that He wants to use *us*.**

However, once we realize He has declared us righteous and given us the status of son-ship or daughter-ship, we know we really do have access to God. And once we realize He has gifted us for ministry, given us the status of priests and ambassadors, and even given us the mandate to be callers of the not-yet into the now, we know we can and should do His works. This is not just a nicety for us, but a necessity for the cause of the Lord. Those who study the growth of the church have found that if just those in professional leadership did the work of the church, then the church could do little more than maintain the status quo. It is *essential* we all take our rightful places in ministry.

When we realize our call and identity, there is something about it that sinks into our spirits and endues an authority, confidence, and passion to be about bringing God's Kingdom on the earth. It raises up a people that had been less than totally awake and engaged, and it forms them into an army that is hungry for its next opportunity to see the Kingdom of God move.

The First Reformation

As pieces of the puzzle started coming at me at an ever-increasing rate, I suddenly began to realize that all of this was not just a key to the second reformation, but had been the key to the first reformation as well. Let me play back the events leading to the first reformation as Martin Luther had experienced them.

In 1505, the young Martin Luther was preparing to be a lawyer. One day, as he was riding horseback during a thunderstorm, a lightning bolt struck nearby. Being terrified of death and of God's judgment, he cried out, "Help! I will become a monk!" Being faithful to his word, that is the direction he took.

In the monastery, he devoted himself to its disciplines and later remarked, "If anyone could have gained heaven as a monk, then I would indeed have been among them." He made pilgrimages where he tried to gain God's favor by praying his way up a long set of steps. Once, when performing communion, he sunk down behind the altar, afraid of his unworthiness before a judgmental God. He later described that part of his life as one of deep spiritual despair.

Seeing the state he was in, his overseer recommended he preach his way through the book of Romans. This is where Luther made his life-changing discovery. It happened as he came across Romans 1:17:

> For in the gospel a righteousness from God is revealed, a righteousness that is by faith from first to last, just as it is written: "The righteous will live by faith."

Reflecting upon this, it hit me that what Luther found was the righteousness of God. It was about identity! Yes, it was also about how we obtain our righteousness: by grace and through faith. But what Luther had discovered, which he had worked at repeatedly yet could never achieve, was this identity of righteousness. And that changed everything.

At this time the church had taken away the access for people to know both God's grace and the Word that could bring them that grace. The priests were the only ones entrusted to read and interpret the Bible. Furthermore, they used, for their own ends, the longing of the people to have certainty in their salvation, which grace could have brought them. In order to raise money to rebuild St. Peter's Basilica in Rome, the church sold indulgences. The church had theological arguments to justify this, but essentially it was asking for the donation of money in exchange for life in heaven. (The Roman Catholic Church has since apologized for this part of their history. I respect them for that—would that every part of the Body of Christ have the humility to admit past mistakes.)

This infuriated Luther, who found this to be in direct opposition to the truth he had uncovered. So on October 31, 1517, he nailed his Ninety-Five Theses to the church gate in

Wittenberg, Germany, stating his opposition to indulgences and other practices of the church with which he disagreed.

Thus began the Reformation. The reformation became centered around the idea of grace and the Word of God coming into the people's hands. This was rightly so, for these are the avenues by which we obtain all of God's goodness. But, for Luther, what these avenues were *toward* was the righteousness we have in God—our identity. This was the spark of the first reformation, and it is interesting that, once again, it is a highlight of the current move of God. I believe it will be the spark of another reformation.

This was all highly personal to Luther. It made a huge difference in his demeanor. Now he was bold in approaching God's throne of grace and bold in everything he did. He stood up against threats on his life and, when asked by the highest council of the church to take back his teachings, he proclaimed, "I cannot and will not recant."

> **I cannot and will not recant.**

This fierce boldness that came with Luther finally knowing who he was is exactly what is needed in the Second Reformation as well. We, too, must boldly move ahead saying, "I cannot and will not stop."

8
Tenacity

Another tie with the first reformation is tenacity. As mentioned in the previous chapter, this was a hallmark of the first reformation. As mentioned in the first chapter, this is also a hallmark of what God is doing today.

Shortly after the puzzle pieces had started coming together, I had gotten together with my long-time friend Robby Dawkins who invited me to go on a ministry trip with him to the east coast. On the day of the trip, I woke up and discovered that some teenagers had fastened a 4x4 beam to their pickup truck and driven up and down our neighborhood, knocking off more than one hundred mailboxes. I found ours more than two doors down the street. Staring at the beat-up mailbox, I thought, "This ministry trip is going to be good!" The enemy will not try to stop something mediocre.

We need to be tenacious. I want to look at some keys for tenacity in the face of warfare by looking at the story of Gideon. Interlaced in that, I will also bring in the tenacious heart of Martin Luther, especially in the way he wrote his hymn *A Mighty Fortress* in the middle of the most intense warfare of this reformer's life. I am not assigning Luther the same importance as Scripture, but I think it is good to learn from history and take inspiration from one of our leaders.

The story of Gideon is in Judges 6-8. It is set in a time when Israel was overrun by the Midianites, who were so oppressive that the Israelites hid in mountain clefts, caves, and strongholds. Whenever the Israelites planted their crops, the Midianites, Amalekites, and other eastern peoples would invade Israel to steal their food. The story begins with Gideon hiding in a winepress, threshing his grain. Though starting out in fear (both from the enemy, then from the presence of the Lord, then from the mission God gave him), he ended up being an example of one of the most valiant leaders ever to face such overwhelming odds. Here are seven keys for tenacity in warfare gleaned from this remarkable story.

1. Know your identity

The first step in Gideon's transformation from fear to a valiant heart was God speaking into his identity. In Judges 6:12, the angel of the Lord appeared to Gideon and said, "The LORD is with you, mighty man of valor!" (NKJV) Though this may not have been true just yet, when God establishes our identity, the way we see ourselves is what we become.

As mentioned in the previous chapter, the same was true of Martin Luther. The remarkable story of the reformation and Luther's ability to tenaciously face warfare came after his realization of who he was in God.

2. Know that your mission is from God

It is almost laughable what Gideon put God through to make sure it was actually God speaking to him and that God really meant what He said. In Judges 6:17 Gideon replied, "If now I have found favor in your eyes, give me a sign that it is really you talking to me." After that, to verify his mission, he asked for not one, but two signs on the fleece he put before the Lord (Judges 6:36-40). Once this was established, however, Gideon became a man on a mission. And his eyes were on God, the author of that mission.

Luther, too, knew to keep His eyes on God in the battle he faced. His hymn began, "A mighty fortress is our God, a trusty shield and weapon. But for us fights the Valiant One, whom God Himself elected." We need to know there is one fighting for us who is valiant, fearless, and imparts fearlessness. Luther also knew that his mission was really about God's mission—the establishment of His Kingdom: "The Kingdom ours remaineth."

3. Know that the battle is real

It seems that some of the church doesn't know a battle is going on—even the phrase "the front lines of the Kingdom" sounds foreign to them. Often the church is thought of only as a nurturing center—not at all a place for equipping an army to carry out a commission.

To Gideon, of course, the battle was very real. It could be that Israel's condition had arisen slowly in a time of spiritual slumber (Judges 6:10), but now it was evident that they were in serious trouble. We, too, only need to see the state of the world, near and far, to know that the Kingdom is badly needed and that it may take a tenacious fight to move its front lines forward (Matthew 11:12).

Luther, too, knew how real the battle was. He recognized that the battle was spiritual yet having real consequences. Having refused to recant at the Diet of Worms in 1521, he said, "I cannot and will not recant anything, for to go against conscience is neither right nor safe. Here I stand, I can do no other, so help me God. Amen." It is interesting how he realized that true safety was only found in doing the will of God. His stance put him in extreme danger, however. He was excommunicated and made an outlaw. He could well have been killed if he had not been hidden away in the Wartburg Castle. In 1523 two of his supporters were burned at the stake.

4. Know that a strategy in warfare is to strike doubt and fear

The story of Gideon is a fascinating example of how God used strategies of warfare against the enemy. These strategies are tactics which the enemy could use equally as well against us, but here they were being used by God against the adversary. Beginning in Judges 7:13-14, we see the first installment of strategies against Midian. In these verses, Gideon snuck close to the enemy camp just as a man in that camp was telling a friend his dream. "I had a dream," he was saying. "A round loaf of barley bread came tumbling into the Midianite camp. It struck the tent with such force that the tent overturned and collapsed."

His friend then responded, "This can be nothing other than the sword of Gideon son of Joash, the Israelite. God has given the Midianites and the whole camp into his hands." I'm not sure how the friend got that interpretation from the dream, but it resulted in sowing seeds of fear and doubt among the Midianites.

This is the first installment of weapons being employed. The Lord was sowing seeds of doubt into the Midianites' minds. I'm sure we can relate to the enemy using that strategy against us. But here *God* was using it. That got me thinking, can *we* use this strategy to further the front lines of the Kingdom of God? I think we can! When we talk to unbelievers whose minds are set against the reality and character of God, sometimes we can plant a seed of truth to cast doubt into their belief system. It is a *truth*, but creates a *doubt*. So I have dubbed this a "TR-OUT"! When we run into a person who thinks there cannot be a God, for example, we can sow a trout, perhaps telling them about some supernatural work of God we have experienced, and let that swim around in his mind for a while! Eventually these truths are going to cause him to doubt his current belief system.

Luther knew all too well the enemy's tactic of instilling fear, but he would have none of it. In his hymn he wrote, "The world's prince may still scowl fierce as he will. We tremble not, we fear no ill." Yes!! He went on, "And take they our life, goods, fame [respect among men], child and wife, let these all be gone, they yet have nothing won." Luther knew the enemy had no hold on him if he only valued God and His Kingdom and was ready to give up all else.

5. Know that another strategy is to instill confusion and division

Judges 7:21-22 shows God's second installment of weapons (which, again, the enemy often tries to use against us): confusion (lack of communication) and division. "While each man held his position around the camp, all the Midianites ran, crying out as they fled. When the three hundred trumpets sounded, the LORD caused the men throughout the camp to turn on each other with their swords." Due to fear and confusion, the Midianites ended up slaying each other. Fear gripped their hearts, partially because their enemy appeared bigger than it was.

Our enemy, of course, can do the very same thing against us. To stop confusion, we need to be able to communicate well. The enemy is well adept at writing between the lines of inadequate communication and breaking us apart at what started out as tiny cracks. We must realize he is out to divide and conquer. Therefore we must be totally for one another and not let that strategy succeed.

Luther, too, knew of such tactics of the enemy. He wrote, "Deep guile [much cunning] and great might are his dread arms in fight." But "one little word can fell him." One word of God is more powerful than all the power of the enemy. One word, chosen for the situation, can regain communication, diffuse confusion, and reunite us in our mission.

6. Know that yet another strategy is to put us into retreat mode

The story of Gideon's encounter with the Midianites ends in Judges 7:22, "The army fled to Beth Shittah toward Zererah as far as the border of Abel Meholah near Tabbath." The third installment of weapons which God used was to put the Midianites in retreat mode. Although the Midianites still could have taken a stand and won, once they were in retreat mode, their course was set.

When things get bad for us, we can be tempted to think that we should not do ministry that brings a lot of warfare. But if we get into retreat mode, the enemy has us on the run and things are going to get a lot worse! The choice is always ours: retreat or let God come upon us like Gideon.

Luther wrote, "He holds the field forever." The field is where the battle is, and God holds the lines. We are called on the field, not the sidelines. Luther goes on, "He's by our side upon the plain." His presence is with us on the field. If we want to stay where God's presence is, stay on the field.

7. Know that God gives us His Spirit

God had stripped Gideon of any confidence this world has to offer by reducing his army from 32,000 to 300. But God had other plans to make Gideon a confident leader. Judges 6:33-34 states, "Now all the Midianites, Amalekites and other eastern peoples joined forces and crossed over the Jordan and camped in the Valley of Jezreel." Just as the enemy was amassing an attack, the pivotal event of the war occurred: "Then the Spirit of the LORD came upon [Hebrew: clothed] Gideon." This is what made the difference in Gideon and in the battle that he faced. The same is true for us—it is pride to think we don't need to be filled with the Spirit to enter a battle. And this pride will come before a fall.

Luther, of course, realized the same thing, "He's by our side upon the plain, with His good gifts and Spirit." Luther knew his battle did not depend on the number of men involved. The phrase in his song, "Of Sabaoth Lord" refers to a Hebrew word meaning the *Lord of Hosts* or the *Lord of Armies of Angels*. With God we are never in the minority! The weapons of our warfare are not of this world, but have divine power to demolish strongholds (2 Corinthians 10:4). It is the Holy Spirit, who is with us, who moves the lines of the Kingdom forward, in the early church, in Luther's day, and in ours.

Contend!

In the aftermath of the battle, a powerful lesson is found in Judges 8:22-23, "The Israelites said to Gideon, 'Rule over us—you, your son and your grandson—because you have saved us out of the hand of Midian.' But Gideon told them, 'I will not rule over you, nor will my son rule over you. The LORD will rule over you.'" Gideon's motivation all along was to do what God said. This was so much the opposite of Saul, who seemed like a more obvious choice when the people clamored for a king years later. However, a heart for God is everything, and in the midst of battle, taking the reins out of God's hands can be a fatal mistake.

When God is with us, we must forge ahead. I remember one time, as I was doing ministry on the east coast, I was driving along feeling a heightened sense of God's presence. As I slept in my hotel room that night, I still felt Him. However, in the morning I felt the gloom of the enemy. So I said, "Lord, where are you? What happened?"

I heard Him say, "You've been pushing forward the front lines of the Kingdom. Don't you think the enemy is going to push back? But when the enemy pushes back, you must push back even harder."

So I asked, "What should I do?"

At that, I felt His Presence fill me. I don't know how to describe it other than to say it felt like a lion inside of me, roaring from within. So push back is what I did.

> **When the enemy pushes back, you must push back even harder.**

A move of God is now upon us. It is characterized by a reformation in desiring everyone to be used, knowing who we are, recognizing the authority God has delegated to us, and expressing tenacity in the face of resistance.

Are we all invited to be part of it? More than we know.

It's time to rise up. It's time to lead the way, demonstrating a tenacity, a sense of identity, an authority, and the spirit of reformation within us. Don't quit at the first sign of warfare: instead push back even harder. This is a time He wants to raise us up and many others like us.

If, like Gideon, we have the willingness to be used, God will give us a new identity of men and women of uncommon valor. The Spirit will come on us, and we can push ahead, forcefully advancing the Kingdom.

In both Gideon and Luther, one contender took on the enemies of an entire nation. You could ask, "If one contender could do that, what would happen if we all were contenders?"

I say, "Let's find out!"

9
Fellowship with the Trinity

If you were appointed by the president to a cabinet position, nothing would make you realize your identity more, or better know the president's heart, than spending time with the president in meetings of his inner circle. More awesome than the president, however, is God Himself, and the circle He invites us into is overwhelming.

First, let me give a brief introduction on the Trinity. Although the word "Trinity" is not itself in the Scriptures, what it represents is well established there. God is one, yet He is in three distinct persons. Each person is truly God, but they are not three gods—they are one.

Deuteronomy 6:4 speaks of this oneness: "Hear, O Israel: The LORD our God, the LORD is one." Here the Hebrew word for "one" is *echad,* meaning unity—not a count of one. But Scripture also refers to God in three persons. "Therefore go and make disciples of all nations, baptizing them in the name of the Father and of the Son and of the Holy Spirit." (Matthew 28:19). (See also 2 Corinthians 13:14 and John 14.) It is also interesting with "New Testament eyes" to go back to the Old Testament and see the three-fold adulation of the angels in Isaiah 6:3, the three-part Aaronic blessing in Numbers 6:24-26, and how God refers to Himself in the plural in Genesis 1:26.

The persons of the Trinity are similar but distinct. God comes to us as our Father—the One who created us. He looks at us with love, saying, "I created you and I am very pleased with what I made in you." That's your Father. God also comes to us in the person of the Son—the One who wore flesh like ours and felt what we feel. He came and perfectly revealed what God is like. He took our sins upon Himself that we might live. He is everything to us; we want to be like Him and we want to be with Him. He is our passion—the Son. In the person of the Holy Spirit we encounter God closely and personally. In this life, this is how we usually experience God's presence. He is so intimate; we share the same breath. Yet, at the same time, He is a wind that is beyond us. God, awesome and close—that is the Holy Spirit.

The Trinity in John 14

My friend George Koch once spoke of John 14 as perhaps the most detailed look into the inner working of the Trinity in all of Scripture. It is such a holy place I call it the "Holy of Holies" of the Bible. Here are some of its verses:

> vv. 10-11a: Don't you believe that I am in the Father, and that the Father is in me? The words I say to you are not just my own. Rather, it is the Father, living in me, who is doing his work. Believe me when I say that I am in the Father and the Father is in me.

> vv. 16-17: And I will ask the Father, and he will give you another Counselor to be with you forever—the Spirit of truth. The world cannot accept him, because it neither sees him nor knows him.

> v. 20a: On that day you will realize that I am in my Father . . .

> v. 26: But the Counselor, the Holy Spirit, whom the Father will send in my name, will teach you all things and will remind you of everything I have said to you.

v. 28b: If you loved me, you would be glad that I am going to the Father, for the Father is greater than I.

In these verses, Jesus describes how intimately the persons of the Trinity dwell with one another. Jesus is in the Father and the Father in Him. The Holy Spirit is with the Father, and He is the One whom the Father sends.

> **In these verses, Jesus describes how intimately the Trinity dwells with one another.**

The persons of the Trinity honor and defer to one another. Jesus honors the Father: "The Father is greater than I." (John 14:28). And in another place the Father honors the Son: "You are my Son, whom I love; with you I am well pleased." (Luke 3:22). Jesus honors the Holy Spirit, calling Him the "Spirit of Truth" (John 14:16), and the Holy Spirit honors Jesus, reminding us of everything Jesus has said (John 14:26).

This humility, honoring of one another, and love toward each other is a model of how we, in the Body of Christ, are to honor and love one another. It is an amazing depiction of unity, a stunning portrait of the interaction of the persons of God.

Note: It is interesting that even nature portrays some of these characteristics of God—it must have given God pleasure to make it so! Two of the fundamental building blocks of the universe are protons and neutrons. Each of these are now known to be made of three even-more fundamental building blocks called *quarks*. Unlike most forces, the force that holds quarks together in groups of three actually becomes stronger the farther they are from each other. Therefore the groups of three are virtually inseparable.

We in John 14

One time as I was reading through this section of Scripture, pondering it all, I came to realize that *we* are also interspersed within these verses:

> v. 17b: But you know him [the Spirit], for he lives with you and will be in you.

> v. 20b: You are in me, and I am in you.

> v. 23b: My Father will love him, and we will come to him and make our home with him.

> **The intimacy within the Trinity is astounding enough, but to find ourselves placed in their midst is almost too much to comprehend.**

Here we find ourselves in this intimate interaction within the Trinity! First in verse 17, the Spirit lives with us and will be in us. Then in verse 20, Jesus is in us and we in Him. Then in verse 23, Jesus and the Father will love us, come to us, and make their home in us. This is not just in heaven after we die, though it will be there, too. Jesus was talking in the context of what would happen soon when He went to the Father (verse 12). The intimacy within the Trinity is astounding enough, but to find ourselves placed in their midst is almost too much to comprehend. That which the persons of the Trinity give to one another—love, honor, and the enjoyment of being with one another—they give to us. We are deeply loved, honored, and enjoyed by God as we dwell in His awesome presence. It was said that President John F. Kennedy's son could come into the Oval Office whenever he wanted and jump on his father's lap. He knew who he was—and how his father loved him. That is God's love for us.

John 14 shows how our life in the Lord involves a closeness with Him. He is available to us all the time, whether coming to Him individually or collectively. It is also true that we, individually and collectively, can grow in this intimacy and in His anointing. We have Him completely, yet there is always more (Psalm 42:1). Just as more encounters with God were in store for the disciples who heard these words, more is in store for us. If we were in the president's inner circle, we can imagine the adventures that would lie ahead as we came to better know the president and were involved in some astonishing situations. The same is true with the Lord. Such is life when we are close to the true and living God.

Partnering in His Work

John 14 takes us into one more facet of this amazing portrait. In it are also these verses which show God's desire to partner with us in His work:

> v. 11b: Or at least believe on the evidence of the miracles [works] themselves.
>
> vv. 12-14: I tell you the truth, anyone who has faith in me will do what I have been doing. He will do even greater things than these, because I am going to the Father. And I will do whatever you ask in my name, so that the Son may bring glory to the Father. You may ask me for anything in my name, and I will do it.

We know that the persons of God partner with each other in their work: Jesus only did what He saw the Father doing (John 5:19) and the Holy Spirit empowered Jesus in His ministry (Luke 4:14). In the same way, however, they want to partner with us.

Ambassadors of the Trinity

Truthfully, this almost seems over the top for me. In this portion of Scripture, unique in showing how the persons of the Trinity interact with one another, why would God put *us* in the picture? And why would He also so exalt the doing of His works (miracles)? Some have felt that we should not pay so much attention to miracles, and not even to ourselves. If it were not for what Scripture says, I might agree with them. But, as John 14 says, this is *God's* idea. The persons of the Trinity show perfect love toward one another. They work together and even bend the laws of nature in order to show us the beauty of heaven manifested here on earth. And they want us to know that we complete this beautiful picture.

It is amazing how we, as mere humans, get to stand with God who created and fills the universe. This alone should cement our identity. It should let us know something of the realm of which we are ambassadors. And it should give us a new perspective of our role in the bringing of His Kingdom—how He partners with us and will do anything we ask in His name in order to show forth increasingly greater works. We are bringers of His presence, those with whom the Most High dwells. Everything about God has a dimension to it that, should He show us its extent, would blow our minds. So it is with who we are, and so it is with what He desires us to do—it is far more than we could think or imagine.

10

Three Elements of Ministry

I have been talking about the components of what I feel is a coming move of God. Now is the time to bring those together in the way we minister to others. This chapter will be just an outline. If you would like to read more on the subject, see my first book *The Presence, Power and Heart of God—Partnering in His Ministry*, which is filled with detail, examples, and tips on how to put everything into practice. In this chapter I would like to lay out, in a concise way, what I think are three major elements of ministering in the Spirit. They are very evident in what is happening in the current move of God, and if you watch any of Darren Wilson's movies, such as *Holy Ghost*, you can see them in action. Those elements are (1) ministering with His presence, (2) listening to His voice, and (3) using His authority. I will also talk about displaying God's heart, which underlies all we do. Part of the identity we have been talking about is being Bringers of the Kingdom, and these are ways to put that into action.

Ministering with His Presence

When I started ministering in this way, I realized two things were radically different from the way I was praying before. First, instead of praying to God "out there," I was asking God to come and for His presence to fill the place. And second, instead of trying to figure out what I should have God do next, I began to ask God what He was doing, so I could do that. The first, of course, is about the presence of God. God's presence underlies everything we do. It makes ministry an exceptionally satisfying endeavor, because we get to do it with Him. It is so vital for ministry that, after His ascension, Jesus instructed His disciples not to do anything until the Holy Spirit He had been talking about showed up (Acts 1:4).

This "showing up" (or coming) of God mystifies some because, they reason, isn't God everywhere all the time? Actually, if you look at all the verses that speak of God being in a place, you can place them into four categories. First, God truly is everywhere all the time—there is no where you can go where God is not there (Psalm 139:7). Second, God indwells believers in a special way (John 14:20). Third, God's presence can come more intensely at times for a specific purpose, such as for healing or to be with us in worship (Luke 5:17, Psalm 22:3). And fourth, at times God's presence can be so overwhelming that our mere human bodies are "overloaded," sometimes to the point of not even being able to stand (Daniel 8:15-18,27, Matthew 17:6-7, Revelation 1:17). Sometimes you or the person you are praying for may sense God's presence like this, sometimes a little, sometimes a lot. (Ask to feel it more—that is one of the things we can grow in.) Regardless of how much you feel it, His presence will make a huge difference in what you are praying for, so welcome His being there.

Besides seeking God's presence for ministry, however, seek God simply to know Him more. God truly is a rewarder of those who diligently seek Him (Hebrew 11:6). The invaluable reward will come in the closeness we experience with Him in our private lives, as well as the times in which we minister. Someone who exemplified this type of seeking Him was Moses. When he first went to Mt. Sinai, people warned him that he could die because God's presence was there. But his desperation led him to go anyway. Having encountered God in the burning bush, his hunger persisted and he asked God to see His presence. God put him in a cleft of a rock and said,

"I will cause all my goodness to pass in front of you ... but you cannot see my face, for no one may see me and live." (Exodus 33:19-20). Even after this, however, Moses' hunger persisted. He must have eventually seen God's face, for later God said, "When a prophet of the LORD is among you, I reveal myself to him in visions, I speak to him in dreams. But this is not true of my servant Moses; he is faithful in all my house. With him I speak face to face, clearly and not in riddles; he sees the form of the LORD." (Numbers 12:6-8). Moses kept pushing the limits and God rewarded him for it. The incident between Jesus and the Syro-Phoenician woman (Mark 7:24-30) is like this in that sometimes it seems God is pushing us away, but He is actually testing our tenacity to come near, and that is what He loves.

> **Upon the invitation, "Come, Holy Spirit," the desire of His heart happens.**

Basically, whether you are alone with the Lord or are praying for someone, ask God to come. He loves that invitation and will certainly give the Holy Spirit to those who ask (Luke 11:13). A Hebrew word for the type of prayer ministry we are describing is *paga*. The root of that word is "meeting." Here we are mediating a meeting between God and the person for whom we are praying. Know that God so much wants to come—He *loves* to come and wants this meeting to happen. Upon the invitation, "Come, Holy Spirit," the desire of His heart happens. He comes. And the meeting, the *paga*, between Himself and the person begins.

Even as I was writing this, Katelyn—a nine year-old prayer team member with a remarkable sensitivity to God—and I were praying for a young woman who was visiting our church. We asked God to come, which happened so powerfully that eventually we realized He was doing all the ministry and there was not much for us to do except watch!

The person was deeply ministered to. Afterwards she said she saw Jesus standing in front of her offering His heart to be placed in hers. In telling my wife about this I said, "Do you know what that means? Jesus was on our ministry team!" In fact, He would love to join all our ministry teams. Ask Him to come.

Listening to His Voice

As I mentioned above, the second thing that made a huge difference in the way I prayed was that, rather than me telling God what to do, I began to ask God what He was doing so I could do that. This is the way Jesus ministered: He only did what He saw the Father doing (John 5:19). And He found that God was ministering constantly (John 5:16). This means, then, that we need to be able to discern what He is doing. Part of knowing what God is doing involves seeing the effects of the Spirit upon a person. But another part is learning to hear His voice.

> **We often need specific direction for specific situations, especially when we want to "do what we see the Father doing" in ministry settings.**

Cover to cover, in over 2100 verses, Scripture shows God talking to man. It is something that God values. Christianity is about a relationship, and in any relationship two-way communication is essential. The Bible, of course, is the main means of hearing from God. It is His clear and undisputed voice and our sole source of doctrine. However, we often need specific direction for specific situations, especially when we want to "do what we see the Father doing" in ministry settings. The Word was not written with the intent of listing step-by-step instructions for every circumstance we might ever encounter. (That's probably not even possible and, even if it were, we often don't know what all the circumstances are.) The Bible gives us invaluable direction and shows us who God is, but in doing so it portrays God as one who will speak to us about specific details in our lives and show us the way. Looking at His relationship with Moses and David, for example, we can see that He loves His people to be close to Him, talking, praying, asking, and listening to His voice. Paul told us twice to earnestly desire to prophesy (1 Corinthians 14:1,39), in which we both hear from God and speak to others what He says. It will, Paul says, strengthen, encourage, comfort, and edify those who hear it (1 Corinthians 14:3-4).

There are a variety of ways God speaks to us. Sometimes He may pop pictures into our minds. Other times He may give us words or Scripture verses. Sometimes we just "know" what God is saying, or He gives us words moment by moment as we start talking to someone. Sometimes we feel physical sensations (such as the pain in someone He wants us to pray for), and sometimes He tells us specifically where to address prayers of command when we are praying for healing. Sometimes we feel His heart beating in ours and give voice to what we are feeling. Other times we may have dreams, see visions, encounter angels, or hear the audible voice of the Lord. There is really no end to the list of ways He can speak to us.

It is important to realize that in hearing from God, there are three parts: the revelation, interpretation, and application. Once you get the revelation, ask God what it means (unless it is obvious). Or sometimes the person to whom you give the revelation will know what it means. As for the application, wait until you have God's heart on it—that is extremely important—without it, it is best to say nothing at all.

In ministering prophetically we sometimes need patience in hearing from God, we often need to take risks, and we always need humility. We must realize that we prophesy only in part and allow people to test what we say. (This is where getting feedback from them is useful.)

If God uses you in this way, teach others how to better hear from God. If hearing God's voice rarely happens at this point in your life, don't worry—it will eventually break through.

Before I started out in this, I was one of those who thought it would never happen to me. I said to myself that if it ever did happen, I would teach others how to do it. But I went for months without getting a thing. Then one day we were in a meeting at someone's home and I was leading the prayer for a man named Darrell who needed prayer for his knee. As we began to pray, I started picturing my riding a motorcycle. I felt guilty for doing so, since I knew we were supposed to be praying for Darrell. But it was such an awesome picture that I had to see what would happen next. As I was driving the motorcycle, I leaned around a curve and sped down a hill. In front of me I could see the road went over the top of a dam. So I glided over the dam and started leaning into a curve on its other side. It was exhilarating! Then, all of a sudden, I saw there was sand on the road and the motorcycle skidded out from under me, spinning off the side of the roadway. Then I snapped out of it and thought, "I'm supposed to be praying for Darrell!" I found the motorcycle ride so intriguing, however, that I decided to tell everyone about it. When I did, Darrell about fell over. That was exactly how he hurt his knee! I was as shocked as Darrell! I found that God does speak to us, although I still was not sure how at that point. Mainly I learned that if God wants to get through to us, He can. He knows how to speak so we can hear.

Over the years, I have found a variety of things that help us hear from the Lord. First, be attuned to the different ways He might speak. Also, earnestly desire to prophesy. Find some friends who are also interested in it and get together. Pick a person to prophesy to and ask yourselves, "If God were here, what would He say to this person?" You will find out God *is* here and His heart is full of things to encourage that person as he or she steps into all God has in store for them.

Using Authority

Authority is the third thing that makes a difference in the way we pray. Because it is so connected with identity and is in the forefront in the current move of God, I devoted Chapter 4 to it. It is the way Jesus prayed. Those extremely short prayers of His were prayers of command. They were not directed toward God, but directed toward whatever needed to be changed, such as a blind eye or lame limb.

I have to admit—the way I am advocating we minister can sound a bit strange to some. First, we are partnering with God who is near, not "out there" somewhere, which, to some, might sound like we have some sort of invisible friend at our side (which we do!). Second, sometimes people think you are crazy when you say you talk to God, but when you say that God answers back, they think you have lost it! And third, I am now advocating that we talk to parts of the body, such as eyes and arms! The only saving grace is that this is the way Jesus ministered. Once He even spoke to a tree and, after that, told us to speak to mountains (Mark 11:12-23)!

So as you pray, especially for healing, use your authority to speak to shoulders to be healed, pain to be gone, and swelling to go down. As I mentioned before, God may speak to you or show you a picture of where to direct these prayers of command.

> As you pray, especially for healing, use your authority to speak to shoulders to be healed, pain to be gone, and swelling to go down.

A story that encapsulates this type of prayer happened at our local public high school. Christina Tammen is an amazing teacher who holds a Bible group that meets once a week after school. Recently I did a series of equipping classes there. In the final session, I talked on authority and healing. Christina had invited some students with injuries to come. One was one of the school's top wrestlers who had severely injured his knee. He didn't know the Lord (yet). He came in a little late just as we were looking for someone to pray for. So the students zeroed in on this wrestler who was standing there on crutches wearing a knee brace. We had a girl who had known the Lord for just several weeks put her hand on his knee. Then we asked the Holy Spirit to come. As soon as we did that, the girl jerked her hand back saying, "What was that? It was like a buzz. Oh, that must have been his cell phone going off!" But we had the wrestler check his cell phone and it had not gone off. So she put her hand back and we kept going.

Everyone was commanding the knee to be healed and the pain to go, and every so often we would have him check his pain level. A method I learned from Robby Dawkins (who learned it from his doctor) is to give a number as to how the symptoms are changing, ten being the place where they started and zero being completely normal. This helps us not to quit too early and also encourages us when things are changing. The pain in the wrestler dropped to a 6, so we prayed again and this time it went to a zero. He had started out in immense pain and now it was gone. He couldn't believe it. Then we started having him check his leg motion. He had virtually no motion when starting. Now he could move it 20 degrees with no pain! Only his knee brace was keeping him from bending it further. The students asked him to take it off. Erring on the side of caution, I said, "Don't do anything against your doctor's orders," but he went ahead and took it off anyway! Now he could bend it 90 degrees with no pain. He was amazed. He started doing deep knee bends. Part of me wanted to stop him, but the other part was saying, "This is so cool!"

Then we had him show us his knee, which was somewhat gnarly looking: swollen with his knee cap off to the side by about an inch. The students prayed again with everyone watching. (These students are SO on fire!) I was standing behind him and could not see, but the students gasped as the swelling went down and the knee cap moved back into place. He got up and walked around, squatting down with no pain! Charlie, one of the students whom I would best describe as a walking revival, said to him, "What God did to your leg He wants to do with your life. Do you want to give your life to Him?"

He said "Sure!"

We went on to pray for another student while he talked to Christina. These students were praying with such authority! The wrestler told Christina that now his biggest problem was not knowing what to say to his coach. Christina told him just to say what happened. She didn't want to miss the coach's reaction, so she decided to go with him to speak to the coach right then and there. Just after they left, Charlie and his friend Jonathan wondered what happened to the wrestler. I told them he was on his way to see his coach. They said, "We want to go too!" and ran off.

They got there just as another wrestler was looking at the one who was healed saying, "What happened to you??!!!"

So Charlie said to him, "What God did with his knee He wants to do with your life." And they led that wrestler to the Lord!

Meanwhile Christina talked to the coach who was amazed, since he was the one who took the wrestler to the emergency room two weeks before and knew how bad it was.

A week later the wrestler visited his doctor. The doctor walked in holding two x-rays, one from when he was injured and one from that day. He said, "I can't explain this!" It was as if he had a new knee.

I am so taken with how much the Lord is upon all of the students in this group. Even a year later, almost every day they are leading someone to the Lord or praying for someone who is healed. The news of who they are in the Lord is going to get out! And it should.

Identity

In all three of these components of ministry, without establishing our identity—without knowing who we are—we will probably be reluctant to step out. As for ministering with His presence, we must know that we are called to be bearers of His presence, those with whom He dwells. As for hearing His voice, we must know that we are answers to Moses cry, "I wish that all the LORD's people were prophets and that the LORD would put his Spirit on them!" (Numbers 11:29). And as for authority, we must know that we have been given it—that we are ambassadors and royal priests.

The Heart of God

If we ask, God will place His heart inside of ours. Whatever we do must reflect His heart. It is a heart for Him that makes us long for His presence. It is with His heart that we must speak His words. And it is in His heart that we pray for the sick, knowing that, moved by compassion, this is what Jesus did continuously. As we speak for healing to come, we are giving voice to our God, who wants His will verbalized as He displays the nearness and goodness of His Kingdom.

> **I want to minister in His personality!**

More and more it has been my quest to better know His heart so that I may better reflect Him. I want to minister in His personality! So, what kind of personality did He have? We know people would come in droves and sit all day, often with nothing to eat, just to hear Him talk. They couldn't stay away! He spoke words of truth and life. They knew His authority was different from anything they had ever known. His miracles demonstrated His compassion and the reality of what He said about His Kingdom. There was life in His eyes.

They could feel His heartfelt passion for their well-being—how much He loved them. Everyone was special to Him. He wanted them to know the beauty of the Kingdom He was there to offer. It pained Him to see the trouble they were in—suffering in a broken world, strong-armed by the hand of the enemy, and in danger of eternal death. He wanted to pull them from this into His Kingdom, where they would be safe and know true life, light, freedom, truth, and joy. All of these things give us an idea of what His personality is like. I realize that each of us is different and will reflect different aspects of who He is, but if we can get close to being like Him, people will encounter Him and get an idea of who He is.

I know when people encounter the heart of Jesus, even when reflected in the heart of believers, it can change lives. Lord, let it be—let the world know You have sent the Son and let them discover how good He is.

11
Ministry in the Last Days

I feel a sense of urgency in bringing this ministry, and the Second Reformation, to the church. What I am about to share is a prophetic sense of what is coming. But even if I get some of the details wrong, I know for certain that this reformation and all it entails is God's heart and is badly needed.

The Last Days

When I say "Last Days," I'm not saying that the second coming of Jesus is at our doorstep. (Although one never knows, maybe it is!) I'm using it in the same sense as Peter—if he could say he was living in the last days (1 Peter 1:20, 4:7), we are more "last" than he was. Simply put, we, like Peter, are living knowing every moment counts. I realize that the interpretation of end-times prophecies have led to much debate and division, sometimes over the smallest of details, and I don't want to get into that here. What is truly important is to be looking to the Lord and doing all He told us to do before He comes. That I do want to get into here.

Like the events God has orchestrated in the past, I believe the events near the time of Jesus' return will have many foreshocks. Many of these the world has already experienced, and I am sure there are more to come. Are the foreshocks increasing? Yes, in many ways they are. Although this itself does not provide us with an end-times timeline, it should remind us to be about our commission.

Current Discussions

Even among those involved in the move of God which I have been talking about, there are differences of opinion in how to talk about the Last Days.

Some seem to rarely mention it. In listening to their point of view (please note that I have not heard any pointed talks on the subject, only remarks on the side), the heart attitude behind it seems to be a frustration with the church's tendency to retreat into inaction whenever the Last Days are considered. I can see their point. In the past, whether talking about the earth being shaken or the Book of Revelation, the church has often retreated into spectator mode, as if there is nothing to do at that point. I think it is just the opposite.

Others seem to dwell on the Last Days often, reflecting the voice of the Spirit and the bride who cry, "Come!" (Revelation 22:17). But can't the entire church do this *and* move more and more into action? I say, yes we can.

> **If the call is to go into action, I'm in.
> If it is to go into spectator mode, I don't see it.**

The same blend is echoed in many of the prophetic voices of our day. Some see (often with unprecedented prophetic experiences, I might add) a coming revival. Others see a shaking. Many are seeing both, as expressed by Isaiah 60:2: "For behold, the darkness shall cover the earth, and deep darkness the people; but the Lord will arise over you, and His glory will be seen upon you." (NKJV). I agree with the latter. However, again the question is: what are we to do about it? If the call is to go into action, I'm in. If it is to go into spectator mode, I don't see it. Yes, John 9:4 speaks of a night coming when no one can work, which may refer to us as individuals when we enter our rest or to a ferocious battle just before Jesus returns. But we are called to fight valiantly until we can fight no more, and we are not at that point yet.

Another Piece of the Puzzle

Throughout this book, I have been describing pieces of a puzzle the Lord has been giving me for several years now. One of the most intriguing pieces came through the young daughter of a pastor friend. I'm not trying to sway any doctrine based on this—I share it with you simply to provoke thought. I honestly do not know where to file it in a theology of the end times. Personally, I'm just trying to follow the Lamb wherever He goes. But there are too many details about this story which are far beyond coincidence not to consider what is being said.

In November 2012, my friend's daughter had the first of two experiences with the Lord. This was not a near-death experience; she was simply lying in bed when she was taken on a visit to heaven. As she approached heaven, Jesus shouted out her name with great excitement. Then she joined Him and a group of other children. He was teaching them, but also playing games and making them laugh. I'm sure there are some who would take offense at such a mundane view of the Lord, but I know that with my own grandchildren, one of the ways I express my love is getting down at their level and taking part in silly games. And who can out-love Jesus?

A month later she had a second experience. This time Jesus came to her, sat on her bed, and explained that she could not make any more trips to heaven for a while because a war had started there. He was kicking Satan out of heaven and, when he came to earth, he was going to be very mad and do some terrible things, especially to children.

In the light of her first experience, I immediately thought that the enemy's plan was to come against those whom Jesus especially loved. Her father, not quite knowing what to do with all of this, called the children of his church forward and prayed for them. Within a week came the first in a series of horrific attacks against children, this one at Sandy Hook Elementary School. Since then there have been other school shootings, kidnappings of school children in Nigeria, and barbaric killings by ISIS of Christian children in Iraq if they did not renounce their faith.

When my friend's daughter told her parents about these experiences, they found many aspects of what she said stunning. One of the things Jesus told her was that a missionary friend would not be able to sail his boat for a while because a storm was approaching. The very morning she said this, her father received an email from this man saying he could not sail his boat out of Palau because a typhoon was imminent.

There were other things Jesus told her that I don't feel at liberty to share. Needless to say, one only need keep up with current events to see the darkness getting darker. But, as Isaiah prophesied, the light upon us is going to be getting brighter.

The part about kicking Satan out of heaven made me start dwelling on what this meant. The language is very similar to Revelation 12. So that is what I will dig into next.

The Book of Revelation

The Book of Revelation was written by John when he was in exile on the island of Patmos. Basically, the book shows how God is in control and that everything will turn out as He planned it. It consists of seven visions. Most start by giving us a view of what is going on in heaven. And whatever happens there then affects the earth as God shatters Satan's realm, sometimes violently. As I mentioned before, Revelation ends

Ministry in the Last Days

with a view of heaven astonishingly similar to the piece of heaven God created in the Garden of Eden, as described in the first few pages of the Bible. But between these glimpses of heaven, spanning from Genesis to Revelation, is the story of our redemption, won by a humble King now coming in fiery victory.

Revelation has provoked many questions as to how to approach and interpret it. Is the book literal or highly symbolic? Is the order of events linear or cyclic (that is, does it often cycle through the same events but from different points of view)? Does it pertain only to the last seven years before Jesus' return, or is it just a symbolic way of looking at the battles and authority of the church in the days between Jesus' first and second comings? (I like the part about our authority, but I don't think it is simply symbolic.) In other words, is Revelation about the now or the not-yet? In our day, we live in the *now* but see reflections of the *not-yet* in the bringing forth of His Kingdom. However, I believe Revelation is about the *not-yet* (see Revelation 4:1), yet also contains reflections of the *now*.

> **If prophecies in the Old Testament reflected the authorship of a timeless God, it would surprise me if the same were not also true about the Book of Revelation.**

If prophecies in the Old Testament reflected the authorship of a timeless God, it would surprise me if the same were not also true about the Book of Revelation. Looking at it this way, we can draw out remarkable pictures of the end times and, at the same time, gain amazing insights to many of the greatest moments in God's history (including our day) from the perspective of a timeless heaven. (Please note that I am not advocating multiple interpretations of this book. I think it is basically about the end times, but it reflects God's timeless touch in tying together many significant events throughout history as it tells us what is to come.)

To show how this works, consider Revelation 5. Notice how future events are tied to what happened before.

> Then I saw in the right hand of him who sat on the throne a scroll with writing on both sides and sealed with seven seals. And I saw a mighty angel proclaiming in a loud voice, "Who is worthy to break the seals and open the scroll?" But no one in heaven or on earth or under the earth could open the scroll or even look inside it. I wept and wept because no one was found who was worthy to open the scroll or look inside. Then one of the elders said to me, "Do not weep! See, the Lion of the tribe of Judah, the Root of David, has triumphed. He is able to open the scroll and its seven seals." Then I saw a Lamb, looking as if it had been slain, standing at the center of the throne, encircled by the four living creatures and the elders. (Revelation 5:1-6a)

It is interesting that at first they could find no one worthy to open the scroll. Why didn't they think of Jesus immediately? We must realize that John had stepped into the heaven of a timeless God. It was as if the events of the past happened only yesterday, standing as vivid as when they first occurred. Even the worship in Revelation 4:8 speaks of the span of all time: "Holy, holy, holy is the Lord God Almighty, who was, and is, and is to come." Looking for someone worthy to begin the end times brought the vivid recollection of another time, a time when God had looked for a solution for fallen man. It was a love for mankind so deep that it drove God to send His one and only Son. Though it happened long before, the very emotion of God's fervor to save humanity from death was still in the air. John feeling this, wept repeatedly. It was as if heaven were doing a passion play to open the new season of things to come.

Ministry in the Last Days

In verse 5 the focus shifted to Jesus' triumph on the cross, and the elder pointed to the Lamb who had been slain. Heaven sang:

> And they sang a new song: "You are worthy to take the scroll and to open its seals, because you were slain, and with your blood you purchased men for God from every tribe and language and people and nation. You have made them to be a kingdom and priests to serve our God, and they will reign on the earth." (Revelation 5:9-10)

Even though the purpose of John's revelation was to show what was to come, the atoning death of Jesus is a pivotal moment in all of history, vivid and real in every age to come. The first and second comings of Jesus are very much sewn together in God's mind, which this revelation shows. (It is also interesting that this vision involves a scroll, and the ministry of Jesus also began with the reading of a scroll. See Luke 4:16-21.) (It is notable, too, that this high song of heaven, proclaiming the wonder of Jesus' sacrifice, also speaks of our resulting identities: a kingdom and priests to serve our God. That shows the emphasis God puts on this amazing fact.) So we see in these verses how the not-yet is tied together with what has come before—it is one magnificent story.

Revelation 12

Now to Revelation 12. It begins this way:

> A great and wondrous sign appeared in heaven: a woman clothed with the sun, with the moon under her feet and a crown of twelve stars on her head. She was pregnant and cried out in pain as she was about to give birth. Then another sign appeared in heaven:

an enormous red dragon with seven heads and ten horns and seven crowns on its heads. His tail swept a third of the stars out of the sky and flung them to the earth. The dragon stood in front of the woman who was about to give birth, so that he might devour her child the moment it was born. She gave birth to a son, a male child, who will rule all the nations with an iron scepter. And her child was snatched up to God and to his throne. The woman fled into the desert to a place prepared for her by God, where she might be taken care of for 1,260 days.

And there was war in heaven. Michael and his angels fought against the dragon, and the dragon and his angels fought back. But he was not strong enough, and they lost their place in heaven. The great dragon was hurled down—that ancient serpent called the devil, or Satan, who leads the whole world astray. He was hurled to the earth, and his angels with him. (Revelation 12:1-9)

The dragon, which verse 9 identifies as Satan, lost his place in heaven. But what is the time frame of these verses? Are they describing the days before the creation of man when Satan, once one of heaven's leaders of worship, rebelled and lost his place in heaven taking a third of the angels with him? Or are they describing the first coming of Jesus, since the "ruler with an iron scepter" of verse 5 is a Messianic reference, like that in Psalm 2:9? Or are they describing a battle in the last days? Actually, all are true. Again, we have a vision from the timeless God, seamlessly sweeping through all history to give John an overview of the battle now taking place. So part of this vision is to come, and part of it is placing it in the perspective of a large sweep of history.

Verse 9, in particular, speaks of Satan being hurled down. Certainly this happened in antiquity. But it certainly also happened when Jesus died and rose again (Matthew 28:18, Ephesians 4:8). And it will happen in the last days, since that

Ministry in the Last Days

is what this revelation is about. Thus, the loosening of Satan's grip seems to be progressive. The works of God's people are also seen to loosen this grip. As Jesus sent out the seventy-two to do His works, they came back with joy at what had happened. Jesus replied, "I saw Satan fall like lightning from heaven." (Luke 10:18). Strangely, what we do on earth can have an effect on the enemy's position in heaven. (See also Revelation 12:11.) The things we do can shake the heavens. (I believe the same can be said of worship, as heaven meets earth and earth meets heaven.)

> Jesus replied, "I saw Satan fall like lightning from heaven." Strangely, what we do on earth can have an effect on the enemy's position in heaven.

I would also like to mention the woman giving birth in this passage. For Jesus, she was likely the nation of Israel (see Genesis 37:9 for matching symbolism). Yet, there are also parallels to the age in which we live. Now *we* are participating in the birth of the Kingdom. And just as Israel is Satan's sworn enemy (even now), the same can be said of us. We were born into this war (Revelation 12:17). I am not saying that we have replaced Israel in God's plans, but rather stand alongside her in them. Although Moses' covenant of the Law was replaced with the New Covenant, the promise made to Abraham (in Genesis 12 and 15) stands unchanged forever. As to the Last Days application, I believe that in the future (based upon Romans 11) this will all be tied together as the Jewish people recognize, in great numbers, that their Messiah is Jesus and join in the birthing of His amazing Kingdom and in our yearning for Him to come.

On December 29, 2012, at the very time I was pondering these things, I tuned into the live web-stream of IHOP's *One Thing* conference. Alan Hood was the night's speaker. And he started talking about, you guessed it, Revelation 12. One thing he said, which I found intriguing, is that as Satan is hurled down, he is removed from his high ground. In other words, things on earth may get worse, but the heavens are freed of his influence, which Revelation 12:10-12 casts in a very positive light. In any battle, having the high ground is an advantage. This again reminded me of Isaiah 60:2. As the enemy leaves his high position, he and his underlings now work through influencing individuals on the earth, but freedom in the heavens (which, in a sense, is where we dwell) is greater than ever. So darkness covers the earth, but the light over God's people is increasingly brighter. Alan's inference was that this is a time of unprecedented opportunity for ministry. (This is not saying that God is not fully accessible today—we can and should have times where heaven is poured out and where healing and personal ministry flow like water. This is talking about a shift in the heavens which brings about far less resistance in the spiritual realm. When an air battle is won, it opens up new avenues for work on the ground, and this needs to be taken advantage of. So minister *both* now and then!) The point is, even in the Last Days, if we see darkness getting darker, it is a call to shine, not a call to retreat.

Revelation 12 continues:

> Then I heard a loud voice in heaven say: "Now have come the salvation and the power and the kingdom of our God, and the authority of his Christ. For the accuser of our brothers, who accuses them before our God day and night, has been hurled down. They overcame him by the blood of the Lamb and by the word of their testimony; they did not love their lives so much as to shrink from death. Therefore rejoice, you heavens and you who dwell in them! But woe to the earth and the sea, because the devil has gone down to you! He is filled with fury, because he knows that his time is short." (Revelation 12:10-12)

Note how this speaks of a time of salvation, power, Kingdom, authority, and overcoming—all on the heels of the enemy and his accusations being thrown down, and all at a time of trouble on the earth. (Again, note our part in this battle.) (It is also interesting, in light of the timelessness of God, that it says that Satan's time is short!) Even though this is a look at the end times, like other prophetic scriptures there are similarities to (and lessons to be learned in) other time frames. Certainly salvation, power, Kingdom, and authority describe the time of Jesus' first coming. It is also true in our day, because Jesus has called us to usher it in. And it will be true in the Last Days, because that is what Revelation is about. Basically, these verses are showing that, even when things on earth get bad, Kingdom, power, and authority are at hand—it is a pattern now and in times to come.

> Even when times are hard, do not fear or retreat ... these may be times of the greatest ministry ever.

The message in all of this is clear: even when times are hard, do not fear or retreat. Be ready for hard times, but realize that these may also be times of the greatest ministry ever. One of the ways to prepare is to learn to minister in God's presence now. This is the preparation God is seeking. Rid yourself of anything that stands in the way of a pure heart and God dwelling in your life. Come *now* to know the salvation, power, and Kingdom of our God, and the authority of His Messiah.

Back to Our Future

I don't want to leave this discussion with a focus on the activities of the enemy. Arguing whether or not the enemy is bringing a shaking is a debate you can only have in an ivory tower. If you look globally, that is a given. What is *not* a given, however, is that there is nothing we can do about it. In Aurora, Illinois, where our church is located, area pastors such as Robby Dawkins and Randy Schoof made a concerted effort to pray for and bring God's Kingdom to the city. Darren Wilson's movie *Father of Lights* documented what happened in Aurora when God intervened in a planned gang war. In the year that followed, the murder rate dropped to zero... unheard of in the city's recent history.

But here—and this is where I go out on a limb—I feel our attention needs to turn on what is REALLY going to cause a shaking to the status quo: a coming tsunami of God's Spirit. It will come like a wind from the east to the west, so powerful it will blow down social and religious structures that stand in its way. It will reconstruct our expression of the Kingdom. Some of it will look destructive, but what it constructs will be a beautiful, heart-felt devotion to our King. These will be times of the greatest intimacy with God we have ever known. And the closeness Christians will feel to each other will be so impacting that it will transcend the paltry lines used by denominations to keep believers apart. I'm not saying doctrine will be unimportant—the allure of false doctrines emanating from the spirit of the times will be strong. But this allure will stand light years apart from knowing God as He truly is and knowing the truth that truly sets us free. Trying to ride this wave of God's Spirit will be what we need to do, but even this will be dangerous if we have an arrogant heart. But to the humble who look to Him, it will lead to times of unparalleled life in Him and unprecedented ministry to others. And we will be surprised to see whom this move of God impacts and brings into the Kingdom, as many, many come to know Him.

This is what we really need to prepare for. It is both a revival and reformation. Draw close to Him now. Worship Him. Let Him define who you are. It is important to do this now, for it will be hard to see in the wind. But remember, you were born for such a time as this.

The Wedding of the Lamb

Having talked about the amazing identity and calling we have in God, and looking at these from so many different angles, I would like to end this book with an experience I had on a plane flying to the eastern United States where I was going to speak on these very things. I was seeking the Lord on the flight, partially because I wanted words from Him for these particular people, but also because there is something about knowing that 1/8 inch of aluminum separates you from a -70 degree Fahrenheit wind traveling at 500 mph that makes you *want* to seek Him! What I started getting was a picture of the wedding of the Lamb (Revelation 19:7), to which Jesus has invited us all.

I remembered several weddings I had attended and how interesting it is that everyone turns to the bride as she walks in. And I remembered the expression on the face of the groom as he watched his beautiful bride walk toward him, a moment he so often dreamed of, now a reality. In thinking about the wedding in heaven between us and Jesus, I was imagining the same things. Can you see all the beautiful angels in heaven turn towards us in wonder as they see *us* on that great and wonderful day? They are taken by our beauty, although we know we have been made beautiful by the magnificence of our King. And then we see the face of Jesus, staring at us with such affectionate love in His eyes, the object of His long-time dream. If you can picture what that face must look like, know this: that is the face that is looking at you now.

That is the very face we want to reflect to the world. They must know that for them to take part in this wedding is Jesus' desire and lifelong dream. The world needs to see His eyes in our eyes and feel His heart in ours. This can happen if we love Him. We will become like the one we love and behold. Perhaps this is the greatest identity we are privileged to carry—being a reflector of the compassionate, loving eyes of Jesus to our world.

The day we take part in that great wedding, we will know without a doubt who we are... beloved of the King. That is who we are today, too. Hold onto this, and to every identity God has given us. The world and the enemy will try their best to strip our true identity from us, leaving us not knowing who we are. But it is of utmost importance to hold on, for this identity reflects who He is. With this identity, it is *He* whom people will behold—Jesus, who Himself reflected the very nature of the Father. This is the One who, through us, will continue to touch people's lives, heal them, speak to them, astound them, rescue them, love them. To be used in this way is the privilege of us all. What we will experience will be extraordinary—all because Jesus is an extraordinary King, yesterday, today, and forever.

Appendix

A Tale of Two Sisters

To give you a sense of how all of this works, I asked two of my daughters to write about their journey in establishing who they are. As they were growing up, they were very different. Holly (our oldest) was always very confident and outgoing. That didn't mean, however, that she didn't need her identity shifted onto something far more wonderful. Mandy (our youngest) was usually very shy—but not anymore. The Lord transformed her into a very different person. Her boldness sometimes surprises me.

Holly's Story

I grew up in the Church, and I remember hearing time and time again, "your identity is in Jesus," or "you can be at rest just knowing you are God's child." I even had something hanging in my bedroom for years that said "I am a child of God." So my identity was staring me in the face, all the time. And each time I'd hear this teaching, I'd nod in assent, thinking I had already learned it. But it wasn't until I was in my twenties that I realized I had never really learned it at all. I think it's like that with a lot of things in Christianity. We hear the same thing over and over, and think that just because we've heard it before we know what it means. But so often we don't stop to wonder whether we ever really learned it the first time. While growing up in the Church I was also growing up in the world. And like it or not, my identity in Christ was residing in my head, while my identity in the world was ever-evolving in my heart. I was a straight-A student until the day I graduated high school, and with every praise from parents and teachers and every jealous glance from my peers, my identity was taking shape. I was the smart girl. I always tried to be a nice, good person; and with every commendation for succeeding in these efforts, once again an identity was being formed. I was the good girl. And sure, I was God's child, too. But which identity really mattered most to me? I didn't realize it until the identity I had built for myself was shaken. I eventually began a career in healthcare, and one day I had a patient who thought I was ignorant and disrespectful and mean. I remember that being the last big straw on top of many little disappointments over the years in people not seeing me the way I thought I should be seen. And on this occasion I just broke down. I could no longer handle being misunderstood. But I knew I wasn't supposed to feel that way, so I began to question why I did.

At that point the Lord showed me what had really formed my identity. I saw myself clinging to a mountain of my talents, attributes, accolades, and accomplishments. It was my identity. And I saw Jesus there, wanting me to take His hand. But I could only do so by letting go of my mountain. I was so hesitant to do so; this mountain was so familiar. It seemed so good. It was built from the way I was raised, to do what's right and good and excellent and reject what's wrong. It was all I knew. Was I wrong? Should I not have allowed praise and correction to shape me? No, I most certainly needed those things. But they were like random pieces of a building all dumped on top of one another in a pile, rather than built onto an already-existing foundation. I had as my identity a messy mountain that could crumble easily at the slightest breeze despite my weak attempts to cling to it and hold it together; what I really needed was a building with a firm foundation that wouldn't slip away when the storms of criticism and misunderstanding rolled in.

So I asked God to show me what I was missing, what I needed to know in order to let go of my mountain and take His hand. And at that point he reminded me of how in kindergarten, I would write and illustrate stories, then show them to my teacher, who would then have me show them to the school principal. My principal would then commend me for my talent and creativity, and then get out his special stamp: a smiley face with a mustache, just like the one on my principal's smiling face. It was his seal of approval. I remember working hard for that stamp, and having no greater joy than to have my work handed back to me with that smiling mustache-face on it. But then the Lord showed me that He too has a stamp, and He too stamps that with which He is well pleased. He marks it with His image, His seal of approval. But He didn't stamp my stories or my homework or even my college diploma. He stamped me. He marked me with His image before I was even born. He approved not my work, but my existence. My very being. And when I messed it up and smudged His image, He undid all of that on the Cross and restored and redeemed everything. That was my real identity. That was my foundation. That was the truth I needed in order to let go of the reputation I had built for myself and take the hand of Jesus and really follow Him. Now I knew what I had heard my whole life about finding my identity in Him. And I've never been the same.

Mandy's Story

Identity has never come easy for me. I wanted it to—I wanted to just move on from it and know who I was already, but God had a different way, as usual, and, as usual, I'm glad that He did. I grew up as a timid little girl, youngest of three, the shyest among anyone I knew. And people didn't mind commenting on how shy I was either. "Why are you so quiet?" or jokingly, "Don't take up all the conversation, Mandy!" I smiled, because politeness is all a shy girl has in social situations sometimes, but inside, any self-confidence I had withered away and my identity became what everyone else perceived of me. If it wasn't shaped by their comments, it was shaped by the enemy who loved beating me over the head with what was spoken and adding his own lies to it. Not having much of a relationship with God, and not being aware that there was a real enemy who lied inside my head, I believed it all and lived my life trying to do my best while thinking I didn't deserve the best anyway. It wasn't until high school when I picked up a book called *Telling Yourself the Truth* that I realized I was doing exactly the opposite, and that maybe the thoughts inside my head weren't my own, and definitely weren't God's.

But the journey didn't end there (and still hasn't). After entering college, I discovered a real relationship with Jesus and found a church home where my faith became my own, and I continued to grow in the Lord. However, identity was kind of a side issue those days. People mentioned things like writing identity statements, knowing the meaning of your name, and finding your calling and giftings, etc. It seemed important, but as I mentioned before, I just wanted to know who I was and move on. Everyone else seemed to have it all together, so I should too. Identity? Check! Next on the list, please? But I kept on running into situations and problems that proved I still had no idea who I was.

It wasn't until about a year ago when I took a three month trip to a missions school in Africa, partially in search of knowing my identity, that I realized how crucial identity really is. I remember my house mom there mentioned in a conversation how most problems in your life are rooted in identity. It was somewhat of a passing comment, but it stuck with me and kept poking at me and proving to be true. When I returned home to America, I began watching a teaching series about the topic as well. It was similar to uncovering a tree's root system which you knew was there the whole time, but had no idea how crucial it was to the condition of your entire tree. And realizing its importance was just half of it! Identity is essential, got it. So what is it then? I had always thought it was something I live *towards*. Become better at this, do more of that, know certain things, feel a certain way. You'll get there! You'll shape who you are eventually! No! Identity is something you live *from*. You are already there, the only thing I had to do was believe, and everything else will flow from that. I already am God's child. I already am saved by the blood of the Lamb. I already am a new creation in Christ. I already am part of the royal priesthood. I don't make my way there by striving, I am there by believing it to be true, because it is! It's true even when I don't feel it, when I mess up and feel like a failure, or when someone comments on how shy I am and I feel unseen and unimportant. My feelings aren't always truth. God has taught me, and still is teaching me, to choose to agree with what He says. I am to hold up that shield of faith which quenches the fiery darts of the enemy, to fight for what I will believe, and to stand on His words about my identity. He invites me into this place of faith, and when I enter into it I become unshakable in the face of my circumstances, a force to be reckoned with in the face of the enemy, and a peaceful, joyful daughter before the face of my Heavenly Father. I am who He says I am, and because of that I am so very blessed.

Bibliography

Dawkins, Robby. *Do What Jesus Did.* Bloomington, MN: Chosen Books, 2013.

Fisk, Randy. *The Presence, Power and Heart of God: Partnering in His Ministry.* North Aurora, IL: Second Ref Press, 2006.

———. *The Amazing Word of God: Partnering in His Ministry.* Libertyville, IL: This Joy! Books, 2010.

Hood, Alan. *War in the Heavens: Session 5 of the One Thing 2012 Conference.* Kansas City: December 29, 2012.

Johnson, Bill. *Face to Face with God.* Lake Mary, FL: Charisma House, 2007.

Kittelson, James. *Luther The Reformer.* Minneapolis: Augsburg Fortress Publishing House, 1986.

Ladd, George Eldon. *The Gospel of the Kingdom – Scriptural Studies in the Kingdom of God.* Grand Rapids: Eerdmans Publishing Company, 1959, 1988.

McGee, Robert. *The Search For Significance: Seeing Your True Worth Through God's Eyes.* Nashville: Thomas Nelson, 2003.

Sheets, Dutch. *Intercessory Prayer.* Ventura: Regal Books, 1996.

Stott, John R.W. *The Message of Ephesians – God's New Society.* Downers Grove: Inter-Varsity Press, 1979.

Wilson, Darren. *Father of Lights: The Movie.* Elgin, IL: Wanderlust Productions, 2012.

———. *Holy Ghost: The Movie.* Elgin, IL: Wanderlust Productions, 2014.

About the Author

After starting out with a career in physics research, Randy has pastored with the Association of Vineyard Churches, taught at Valparaiso University, and, for over 20 years, has focused on helping other pastors equip their people to minister. He has also been a worship leader in the Anglican Church in North America. Randy has spoken, ministered, and taught in various settings, always with an emphasis of having the participants experience the ministry, not just hear about it. His heart is to give away all he has and see the Body of Christ mobilized in effective and empowered ministry.

Randy and his wife, Mary, live in North Aurora, Illinois. They have three daughters, Holly, Becky, and Mandy, a son-in-law, Keith, grandson, Judah, and granddaughters, Rayah and Faith, all of whom are their delights.

Additional copies of this book or Randy's other books, *The Presence, Power and Heart of God – Partnering in His Ministry* and *The Amazing Word of God*, are available through online booksellers such as Amazon and Barnes and Noble. To inquire about multiple-copy discounts, e-mail the author at RandyFisk333@gmail.com.